AF596614

Hold My Juice Box

Hold My Juice Box

Build Your Business, Be a Great Mom, and Stick It to the Doubters.

Olivia Radcliffe

authors
AND CO.

First published in Great Britain in 2024
by Authors & Co.
www.authorsandco.pub

ISBN 978-1-915771-85-8 (paperback)

Disclaimer:
The content provided in Hold My Juice Box is based on the author's personal experiences and opinions. Readers should understand that they are responsible for their own actions and decisions. The author and The Bluebell Group, LLC will not be held liable for any losses, damages, or injuries incurred as a result of implementing the information provided.

For Greyson, my reason behind everything. I am blessed beyond measure to be able to be your mama.

Contents

For additional resources, visit holdmyjuiceboxbook.com

Foreword

“Is that a rainbow bookshelf?!?”

Those were, if I recall, my first words to Olivia when we met on a Zoom call to talk about business. For the record, it absolutely was a color-coded rainbow bookshelf behind her.

There was this air of calm about her that I couldn’t quite wrap my mind around. We were talking about the big goals she had for herself and her business, and how she wanted to shift things over the coming years. Her vision for her success. And like any good entrepreneur with big goals, she was looking for someone who had done it to help her find her way there.

We sat there on Zoom with her perfectly organized rainbow bookshelf in the background as her son popped in and out and asked for help with his tablet, needed hands-on with a snack, and of course, wanted to open a juice box.

There was something about the way Olivia had so much patience for these moments. They could be called “interruptions” in some circles, but not in this one. They were just moments when her little human needed her. She was fully present for him for that second, and then back as quickly as I could snap my fingers—fully present with me.

I knew at that moment that no matter what her goals were, she was going to achieve them. She had something every business-owning mother with kids strives for.

Not balance, no. Frankly, that's near impossible. Sometimes your kids need you more, and sometimes your business needs you more.

No, Olivia had presence.

She was able to calmly and assertively be present with her son, and with her business, moving smoothly and fluidly between roles like she had been practicing at it for decades.

Truth is, I've been at this motherhood and business game for a decade longer than Olivia, and I can't hold a candle to her level of patience and presence with her child. It's something I've aspired to for years. To be able to be fully at the swings when I'm pushing them instead of thinking through pushing out a new offer, fully flipping the pancakes instead of worrying about Facebook posts, fully snuggled up to watch a movie without mentally slotting in that webinar I have to watch later.

While I'm in the stage of parenthood where my kids are coming to me about Wi-Fi passwords and rides to the movies, there she was, having figured out how to drop all of the shame and guilt and mental anguish around being both things—a mother and an entrepreneur—while her little one was still watching Bluey and asking to get pushed on the swings at preschool.

I knew she had a lot to share, and a lot to teach all of us.

In the time since we connected, she has proven me right. Olivia has a lot she can teach all of us about letting go of the social conditioning, the shame, the limitations, the guilt, the things that have us *reactively* switching (and let's be honest, losing our patience sometimes) instead of intentionally moving from one focus to another.

This book is everything I hoped it would be, sharing her wisdom and knowledge to help all of us be not just better entrepreneurs and business owners, but better moms.

Because let's be real. This life is *hard*.

The truth is, most of the "right" ways to do entrepreneurship were written by people who had the privilege of a mother doing the mothering—to them, for them—so they could do the meditation, the morning pages, the hour-long jog before checking emails without a toddler on their lap.

It's hard not to internalize those expectations, but they weren't written for us. They were written for the people who have the benefit of our labor, to make the most of what we gave them.

Our job, then, is to make the most of what we give ourselves.

Olivia teaches us how to do this.

Both how to give to ourselves, and how to make the most of it.

Something I've learned about motherhood and business (which I've been doing simultaneously for the past fourteen years) is that building a business that suits your needs is not optional.

Aside from unschooling and worldschooling three children at home and in our nomadic travels across the western United States, which presents a unique set of requirements… I also have ADHD. I was blessed with the "combined type" of ADHD, meaning that I'm both inattentive and hyperactive. I both can and cannot, at the same time.

Of course, I didn't realize this early on. All I knew was that I was starting my day with a baby in one hand and a laptop in the other, trying to figure out why I could do calls some days and not others… meet some deadlines but not all… do some tasks reliably and others inconsistently…

It wasn't until I was reading a book about resilience twelve years ago that things started to shift for me, because I finally understood that the key to being successful wasn't in *fixing* myself or changing my circumstances. It was in accepting myself and my circumstances and building a business that actually suited them.

I stopped trying to fix all of my weaknesses and instead started playing to my strengths.

I cut down my meeting days to two per week, leaving five days for life, bad brain days, and the flexibility to drop my laptop and head to the waterpark instead.

I shifted my work hours to stop pretending that I was a morning person. Luckily for me, my kids *all* got the sleep-in genes, so we start our days at nine am around here and have for years. I often don't even get into the office until one or two pm if I'm not on calls, spending the mornings sipping coffee, flipping pancakes, and reading *Warriors* or *Heartstopper* or *Diary of a Wimpy Kid*.

I learned to stop when my brain stopped working, and just go play. Pushing through almost never works anyway, so why not build that house in Minecraft or beat your kids in a game of "try not to laugh" for an afternoon instead?

I stopped giving myself deadlines that weren't tied to meetings or external factors because I wouldn't hit them.

I stopped trying to do morning pages and morning exercise and morning meditation and instead decided to do morning mothering, because that's what we needed to do.

I started recording answers to the questions I was asked over and over, meaning I could spend a few hours per week on "office hours" and help all of my clients in less time.

In just over a decade, I went from nursing at the keyboard at two am, trying to copy other people's models for success, struggling even to figure out what I wanted let alone get it... to working sixteen to twenty hours per week, spending eighty percent of that time on things I enjoy, and making more money than I've ever made in my life.

Not because I finally successfully copied someone else's model for success, but because I finally figured out and implemented my own.

I was lucky enough to get an advanced copy of this book to read, so I did—over a weekend, on my tablet, in the sun, watching my kid jump on the trampoline.

Tonight, I sat down to write this foreword with my teenager by my side. He was teaching the dog a new trick, telling me about his friends online and their travels, and explaining how pinning a message on Discord works.

This is what motherhood and business look like for me, but it might be different for you. And that's kind of the point.

So, in form with this book, I'm going to leave you with five actionable takeaways from this foreword as you go on and read *Hold My Juice Box*:

1. Everything Olivia shares in this book is for you to ponder and take what you need from it. I know Olivia, and she is not giving you a prescription for the exact actions to take. This is a set of questions to think about, categories of changes you can make, and circumstances for you to consider. Everything in this book is for you to take what is valuable and save the rest for another time.
2. Read this book in order. A lot of business books allow you to skip over a chapter here and there or

read the good nuggets first. This book builds on itself in each chapter as it goes. Every piece of advice is informed by the one that came before it, giving you a more complete picture as you go. I highly recommend reading it in order.

3. Take notes as you go. Think about your priorities. Grab your highlighter and annotate the important passages you want to remember later. I know I did.
4. Consider Olivia a role model for you, just as you are for your kids. She's not perfect and doesn't claim to be (so don't worry, this isn't a journey of comparison; you won't feel the tinge of shame you get from watching bedtime cleaning routine TikToks as you lay on your pile of unfolded laundry) but she does have wisdom to share from her experience. Relate her stories to your life, and work to apply them to your situations.
5. Be flexible, kind, and patient as you read. Think about the expectations you normally put on yourself when reading a book like this. Do you try to race to the finish? Apply key takeaways while they're fresh? Try to make the most of it somehow? What if, instead, you just enjoyed this book and gained knowledge and insights? What if you read it slowly? What if you allowed yourself to get pulled into other moments, to read other books in between, to come back to this when it calls to you? Give yourself the same kindness, patience, and flexibility to read this book as you want while applying it to your business.

Most of all, take the time to learn from someone who has really figured out some of this motherhood and business "stuff." Olivia truly has something special in these pages, teaching all of us how we can be more present with our businesses and our families. I can only hope one day I'll have this mastered in the way she has.

— Cheryl Woodhouse

Introduction

(aka Pseudo Chapter 1)

The main thing you should know about this book is that this book is chock full of lies.

As moms with businesses, there is a boatload of lies that society has told us—and that we've told ourselves. If you've ever felt hampered on your path to success, joy, and fulfillment, there's a good chance it's because you've been fed (and believed...) too many of these falsehoods.

The lies we're talking about aren't the loud, obnoxious, blatantly obvious lies, waving their red flags defiantly in the air. They're subtle, everyday thoughts that we have been conditioned to believe about ourselves and about what we should or must do with our lives. Lies about what is "good" or "acceptable.'" Lies about what is possible for us to achieve.

These lies are nasty little things that are born from cultural norms, echoed by the media, ingrained by our upbringing, and even whispered by our own subconscious. Day after day, they chip away at our confidence and sense of worth, showing up in the form of pervasive mom guilt, sleepless nights filled with anxiety, imposter syndrome, and a veritable host of other professional challenges from lead generation all the way to maintaining consistent cash flow.

In this book, you'll discover fourteen of the most common lies that keep us moms in business from reaching our true potential. I'll peel back the curtain a bit and share stories of how these lies may be affecting your day-to-day life and undermining your everyday happiness and business success. And—more importantly—I'll share how you can take action and confront these lies, kick them to the curb, and fully embrace the truths that will elevate your life and business to the next level. Because, ultimately, it doesn't matter if you have the best, most well-crafted, absolutely genius marketing and business strategy in the world—if you believe *even one* of these sneaky little devils, you won't ever feel the level of success and fulfillment that you're looking for.

With a couple of decades in the world of marketing under my belt (which is several lifetimes in the digital marketing world, by the way), I know a thing or two about effective, money-making marketing and business strategies. I've worked with companies of all sizes, from solopreneurs to corporations, from all around the world, in different kinds of industries. I've been in the business trenches, building launches with six-figure days and scaling businesses from ground zero to empire status.

I'm also a mom, partner, homeschool teacher, personal chef for picky eaters, chauffeur, perpetual cheerleader, home remodeler, and so much more. Despite the significant success I'd helped others achieve, when I was a new mom, I found myself wrestling with my own inner business demons. I was hustling non-stop, working my booty-butt off (to borrow the term from my preschooler), and yet, it felt like I was running in place. I was pouring my heart and soul into my work, following all the best practices, and applying proven strategies that catapulted *others* to success, yet I was trapped in a cycle of frustration, exhaustion, and unfulfillment. I was checking all the right boxes and doing everything "right," but still, it felt like my turn for happiness and success was always just around the corner, forever out of reach.

That's when I hit pause. I took a deep breath, stepped back, and looked at my life from a new angle. And then I had my quintessential *aha!* moment.

Are you ready for it?

I realized I was chasing someone else's definition of success. I was living a life based on someone else's expectations, not my own dreams. I was ignoring my intuition, my natural strengths (and weaknesses), and the needs of my family, all to try to squeeze myself into a "typical entrepreneur" box. My fear of failure was so intense that I compromised my own boundaries. I was so worried about what others would think or what the critics were saying about how I was showing up as a mom—or as an entrepreneur—that I forgot to show up as *me*. All of this fear and falseness weren't just undermining my happiness, they were sabotaging my success.

In other words, I was letting the lies dictate my life.

Once I saw the light, I didn't hesitate for a second—I flipped the script. Today, as I write this, I can honestly say without a shadow of a doubt that I've never been happier or felt more fulfilled. That's not to say that everything is unicorns and rainbow-sprinkle cupcakes; there are still hardships, hurdles, frustrations, and days I just wish I could roll up in a blanket burrito with a bag (or three) of chips. That's just life.

But I also have middle-of-the-day dance parties with my family, early morning sunrise hikes, the freedom to homeschool or to dive into fun projects (like writing this book!), all without sacrificing my sleep, time with loved ones, or even my guilty pleasure time spent reading cheesy romance novels. I've been able to step away from my full-time job to focus instead on the multiple businesses I own and co-manage and embrace my role as a mom exactly the way I always wanted to.

The next thing I'll tell you is that you can have it all, whatever "all" looks like to you, all on your terms. Want to be a great mom? You are. Want to have a six-figure business? Yours, babe. Want a seven-figure business? Go out and claim it. You can grow a full-time business or a side hustle, work only during nap times or hire a nanny so you can work full-time, breastfeed during business meetings, make a boatload of money while you're sleeping, wake up at two am to batch create your YouTube videos, spend the morning at the park with your kids, hit up the sauna after lunch... the truth? Whatever your own personal dream life looks like, it's possible.

Sound like a pipe dream? Too good to be true? I get it. But mama, that there is Big Fat Lie #1. The doubters will tell you that it's not possible. That you're a bad mom for focusing on your business, or a bad businesswoman who will miss out on sales if you spend the afternoon playing cars instead of sitting at your desk. You'll hear that chasing your "dream life" is just an impossible cliche.

Have you ever felt like you're a bad mom for pursuing your passions or business dreams? Have you worried about what others will think? Have you ever felt that you're not good enough? That your ideas aren't unique enough? Or stared up at the ceiling at night, anxiety etched on your face as you let the fear of failure wash over you? I know I've been there.

In the world of mom entrepreneurs, there's a cacophony of voices—some internal, some external—telling us what we can't do, shouldn't do, or must do to succeed. These voices echo the lies we've absorbed: that pursuing our passions is selfish, that we must make a choice between being a good mom and a successful entrepreneur, or that professional fulfillment is a luxury we forfeited the moment we stepped into motherhood.

I'm not saying it will be easy to release these lies. They've been deeply ingrained in you for pretty much your whole life. But, hey, you're a mom. You do impossible things every day, right? You're nurturing the next generation while running the show in the boardroom. You're raising your kids while striving to make the world a better place.

You're the living embodiment of ambition and resilience, the force that turns kitchen table dreams into thriving businesses while wiping sticky fingers (seriously, why are they always sticky?) and singing lullabies. You're the queen of multitasking, the master of adaptability, and you can turn chaos into cash flow with finesse.

So when the doubters tell you that your "all" isn't possible and serve up judgment with a side of guilt, sleepless nights, and days when all you want is to collapse in bed, stand tall. Pop that baby on your hip, laugh, and simply say, "Hold my juice box," as you stroll off to prove them wrong.

(You may now commence with Actual Chapter 1.)

1
I'm Not Good Enough

Mom.

Is there any word more powerful? The moment your baby breathes out that sweet "Mama" for the first time can make your heart feel like it's going to explode into a million pieces with joy. A panicked "Mommy!" shrieked from somewhere deep in the playground propels you faster than a herd of wild horses. And a drawn-out, exasperated "Mo-o-o-om" combined with an expert eye roll from your teen can send your blood pressure through the roof faster than chugging back-to-back energy drinks.

Moms are nothing short of superheroes (with diaper bags and crossbody packs instead of capes). Often the unsung heroes of the story, moms embody a formidable blend of resilience, compassion, and an unwavering love that defies all logic. That fierce, protective love a mom has for her kiddo triggers a firework show of oxytocin in your brain. This chemical cascade not only nurtures trust, empathy, and connection but has tangible effects on the child's well-being. The mere smell of their mother can help soothe a baby. The sound of her voice can help promote brain growth. A mother can spend around one thousand eight hundred hours breastfeeding—almost the equivalent of a year working a full-time job (minus the vacation days, of course).

But it's not all about biology; you don't have to have given birth to a baby to be a mother. It's about that heart of yours that's all in, ready to sacrifice and show up. It's about that mom strength that's unlike anything else, pushing through adversity over and over (and over) again. It's about creating those moments—from the belly laughs during tickle fights to the tough love during time-outs—that shape your kids into the amazing, inspiring humans they're meant to be.

And yet, despite the day-to-day heroics, another thing most moms have in common is this nagging, relentless, unwavering feeling of *I'm not enough*. Every single mom is out there juggling, balancing, and (to borrow the vernacular of my tween niece) downright slaying it day after day. And yet, there's this pesky, ever-present voice that whispers none too sweetly, "Girl, you are not even *close* to enough."

Let's talk about mom guilt because I don't think I've yet met a mom who hasn't experienced this phenomenon at some point or another. (If you're a mom and you're telling me you've never felt that weight, allow me to offer my heartfelt congratulations and ask that you spill your secret!) Mom guilt is like that uninvited house guest who won't leave but also keeps insisting that you're doing everything wrong. It's a relentless shadow that follows you around, whispering in your ears that you're not doing enough, that you're failing in some way. It's that nagging feeling that no matter how much you do, despite the mountains you've moved today, *it still isn't enough*.

There was one afternoon when my son was just a few months old that I remember like yesterday; it was during the middle of the COVID-19 pandemic, and I had found myself suddenly heaved into life as a new single mom, trying to figure out breastfeeding and how to cut his tiny little nails without giving myself a panic attack, all while working a full-time job and keeping two global businesses afloat from my living room. (Whew. I'm exhausted just writing that!)

It was one of those picture-perfect spring days, complete with sunshine and the smell of lilacs wafting through the house. I was wearing my favorite striped sundress that made me want to twirl like a princess and had just come in from playing with Greyson outside, letting him explore the flowers. Greyson was in one of those "I'll only sleep if I'm being held" phases, so I snuggled him to my chest with a wrap and grabbed my headset so I could jump on a quick call with a potential customer. All was well. I totally had it.

And then the proverbial shitake mushrooms hit the fan.

My German Shepherd, Nola, had taken the opportunity while we were outside to explore the contents of the Diaper Genie, selecting the rankest, most disgusting blowout diaper she could find. I walked down the hallway to find neon green baby poop smeared across the floor and walls, and my dog lightly gagging as she quickly tried to swallow the evidence.

In case you didn't know, those magical crystals in diapers that help keep your baby's bum dry are not so magical in a dog's stomach. So, while cuddling my sleeping three-month-old and without missing a beat on my call, I put on my amateur vet hat and induced Nola to vomit out her diaper snack, while strategically muting myself so no one on the call could hear the sound of my poor dog heaving in the background.

The crisis was averted. Nola was fine. The call went off without a hitch. Greyson didn't even wake up. But I still felt like a complete and total failure. I felt like the worst dog mom (*how could I let her get the diapers?*), entrepreneur (*that was so unprofessional of me*), mom (*I should be focusing more on him*), and homeowner (*my house is literally covered in poop*), all at once. I had gone from smelling the flowers and feeling like I had everything under control to *how could I think I could possibly handle this* faster than you can say "diaper disaster."

Let's be real: we put an enormous amount of pressure on ourselves to always maintain an Instagram-worthy level of perfection. But this isn't just personal pressure—it's a cultural one, deeply rooted in societal expectations that bombard us with images of flawless execution in every role we play, from motherhood to entrepreneurship. This relentless pursuit of perfection is worse than the *Baby Shark* song playing on repeat in our minds, replaying those unrealistic standards that society, culture, and our own past experiences have hammered into us. *Need to be perfect, doo-doo doo-doo doo-doo!*

And let's not forget the double standard that exists for women in the business world. We're constantly battling stereotypes and biases, having to work twice as hard to prove ourselves. So it's no wonder we internalize this belief that we're not good enough, that we don't and can't ever measure up to some unattainable standard of success.

This lie of "I am not enough" can be a continuous dead weight on your shoulders, fueling stress and anxiety, and making you continually second-guess every decision you make in your business, afraid that somehow you'll mess it all up. And, in your personal life, it can lead to burnout, strained relationships, people-pleasing, settling for less than you deserve, and a never-ending cycle of doubt. (Yikes!) The impact of believing this lie seeps into every single aspect of our lives, affecting our mental health, our business decisions, our parenting, and even our personal relationships.

But here's the thing: perfection is a myth, and the enemy of progress. It's an unattainable standard that no one—not even those Instagram-worthy moms with their perfectly curated feeds—can live up to. And yet, we internalize this belief that if we're not doing it all (and not doing it all perfectly) then we're somehow failing.

From a psychological perspective, this phenomenon is often referred to as imposter syndrome—a pervasive feeling of self-doubt and downright fraudulence, despite the overwhelming evidence of success. It's like we're constantly waiting for someone to call us out. We convince ourselves that we're not worthy of success, that we're just playing dress up and pretending to be competent entrepreneurs and good mothers. And, coupled with issues of low self-esteem and feelings of unworthiness, it can create a perfect storm of negative self-talk and limiting beliefs.

But the truth is, you are deserving, you are capable, and you are enough. Recognizing that this lie is just that—a lie—is the first step towards breaking free from its grip. You are more than capable of running a successful business while being a fantastic mother. You don't have to be perfect to be successful. You just have to show up and give your all, even if your all at the time is less than one hundred percent.

Ultimately, when you can fully and deeply accept yourself for who you are—flaws, weaknesses, strengths, quirks, accomplishments, setbacks, pet peeves, experiences, and more—you will open up a whole new world for yourself. I have this little self-worth exercise that I absolutely adore: whenever I do something that I would typically judge myself on, I simply smile and say, "Oh, that's just so Olivia!"

For example, I'm a notoriously bad cook. I *can* cook, but I get too impatient and try to speed things up and skip steps. Like when I turned the heat on too high when cooking rice and somehow permanently melded the rice and the pot together. Or when I set scrambled eggs on fire. Or when I *somehow* melted a frozen pizza into a burned blob at the bottom of my oven. (Yes, I have ruined frozen pizza. It's that bad.) So, the other day, when I got impatient and was a little (ok, a lot) heavy-handed with the salt in the stir-fry I was making, I was able to laugh right along with my family as we ordered takeout instead.

There's magic in that moment, a sense of liberation that comes from embracing your unique self—flaws, quirks, and all. It's all about recognizing that you're perfectly imperfect, and that's more than okay. That exercise is a reminder to myself that I am who I am, and that's something to celebrate. Because let's be real, we all make mistakes—and I mean all of us. It's perfectly normal and part of being a growing, learning, progressing human. I'd hazard that if you don't screw up at least a little every now and then, you're probably not really living life.

What really matters is what you do *after* those slip-ups. Do you beat yourself up endlessly? Or do you choose instead to show yourself grace and learn from the experience? It's about acknowledging—and even embracing—our flaws and using them as opportunities for growth.

We all have our own unique set of strengths and weaknesses. Maybe you actually are a master chef in the kitchen, whipping up mouthwatering meals that your family devours... but cleaning the bathrooms is your downfall. Or perhaps you're an absolute whiz on social media, creating viral content left and right... but you get major writer's block when it comes to your emails. When we compare ourselves to others without considering these differences, we're setting ourselves up for unnecessary feelings of inadequacy. Instead, celebrate your individuality, embrace your strengths, and work on improving your weaknesses without judgment.

My worth is innate. *Your* worth is innate. Your worth is separate from your achievements, how many people are on your email list, or whether anyone even saw your last social media post. Your accomplishments or goals or dreams in life don't make you worthy, either. You are worthy. Period. Exactly as you are, right now, sitting there at this moment reading this book. Enoughness is an inside job. If you don't feel enough, then nothing you ever do will be enough or make you feel enough. It will just be a continuous hustle, driving for more—more love, more money, more success—day in and day out, continually moving the goalposts and never actually accomplishing your goals.

One of the earliest parenting tips I was given that has stuck in my brain ever since was to make sure that you encourage your kids to be proud of *themselves*, instead of simply saying how proud you are of them. Initially, this bit of advice felt odd to me; don't I want my kid to know I'm proud of him? But over the years, I've come to see the wisdom in it. Yes, it's important for your kids to know you're proud of them and love them unconditionally. But it's also crucially important that they love *themselves* unconditionally. Maybe if we can teach our kids to know their own internal worth versus continually seeking external validation, we can end this cycle of feeling not enough.

I wish I could put a magic Band-Aid on your enoughness wound and make you feel better as quickly as a Paw Patrol Band-Aid can help my son's ouchies. But, as we've said, enoughness is an inside job. The most I can do is bring this lie into the light so you can see it for the monster it truly is.

Unfortunately, like so many other women, I have a history of abuse in my life. For years, I believed the lies my abuser had told me: I wasn't good enough; no one liked me; I wasn't smart enough; I wasn't pretty enough; I wasn't worthy. I repeated their words so often to myself that I didn't even realize that their words had become my own. When I finally realized what I was doing, *years* after I escaped my abuser, it shook me to my core. I made the decision there and then to intentionally speak words of love to myself instead of the hate and judgement I had mentally been spewing throughout the years. I looked at myself in the mirror and, instead of tearing myself down, I told myself how amazing I was. I gave myself compliments. I even high-fived the mirror.

And, let me tell you, it felt incredibly stupid. It was hard and silly and felt pointless, mainly because I didn't believe what I was saying to myself—yet.

But I kept at it, and eventually, I noticed that it felt just a teensy bit easier. The compliments were more genuine. It felt more natural to bring my strengths into the light, and, even more impactfully, to acknowledge and embrace those things about myself that I used to hide desperately from others. Like the fact that I can be a horrible cook. I'm a gigantic nerd. I sometimes find social engagements downright painful. I have stretch marks and my belly looks like a deflated balloon. I'm horrible at team sports and really would rather do pretty much anything else. I have two fake teeth that are a slightly different color than the rest of my smile. I have "overly large" kneecaps (according to my chiropractor).

But I began to embrace the truth: I am enough, unconditionally, exactly as I am. Stretch marks and overly large kneecaps and all.

And the same is true for you. The next time you find yourself falling into the comparison trap that you've set for yourself, pause and remember: you are uniquely you, and that's your superpower. Embrace it, own it, and watch as you open up a whole new world of self-acceptance and empowerment. Remind yourself of all the amazing things you've accomplished, all the challenges you've overcome. The most successful people aren't the ones with no flaws who never fail—they're the ones who never give up.

Take Action

1. ***Create a Hype File.*** Take a moment to reflect on some of your accomplishments so far—your achievements, rave reviews, compliments from others, etc.—and write them down. Did you successfully launch your business? Did you manage a tough client situation (or toddler situation) with grace? Celebrate those victories. Seeing your achievements on paper can be a powerful reminder of how far you've come.
2. ***Break down goals.*** Break down your big goals into smaller, manageable steps. Sometimes, the feeling of not being good enough comes from setting unrealistic expectations. Focus on what you can do this month, this week, today, or even just in the next hour. Progress, not perfection, is what matters.
3. ***Practice self-compassion.*** Be kind to yourself. You're juggling a lot, it's okay to make mistakes. When you slip up, talk to yourself the way you would to a friend. Give yourself grace and remember that every setback is a setup for a comeback. Treat yourself with the same kindness and understanding you offer to others.
4. ***Surround yourself with positivity.*** Your environment has a significant impact on your mindset. Now, this doesn't mean you have to always be happy and surround yourself with unicorns and animated, singing birds (unless that's your thing, of course!). Do focus on surrounding yourself with positive influences. Follow inspirational accounts on

social media, read motivational books, and listen to uplifting podcasts. Fill your world with voices that lift you up and remind you of your worth.

5. ***Affirm your worth.*** Create a list of positive things you would like to believe about yourself and repeat them daily. Phrases like "I am capable," "I am enough," and "I'm a badass mom who is slaying it with my business!" can rewire your brain to believe in your own value. Stick them on your mirror, your computer, your phone lock screen—anywhere you'll see them regularly.

Despite the messiness, the chaos, and the moments when you feel like you're barely holding it together, you're doing the best you can with what you've got. And that, my friend, is something to be proud of. Don't let the lie hold you back from your true potential. You are strong, you are capable, and you are more than enough.

And you've got this.

2

I'm a Bad Mom

Last night, I had a dream that, for some unknown reason, I dropped my sleeping four-year-old off at a bar. And walked away. Just like that.

In the dream, when the realization hit, I was engulfed in a frenzy to get back to him (with all sorts of impossible and maniacal dream hurdles in the way, of course). The mental flagellation I gave myself, even in a dream state, was nothing short of vicious. And—shocker—when I woke up drenched in a cold sweat and heart pounding, I continued to beat myself up mentally. *Why would I even dream that? What does that say about me as a mom? Clearly, I must be a bad mom.*

Being a mom is a never-ending series of decisions. What they eat, what they wear, who they play with (who they *don't* play with...), screen time, bedtime, bath time... It's a never-ending checklist.

And a never-ending list of ways to feel like you're failing as a mom.

This feeling, dare I say it, becomes compounded when you're a mom building a business alongside raising your Littles. Inevitably, you'll find yourself in that gut-wrenching moment when you have to choose between answering your kid's puppy-eyed plea to play with them or answering the call of a looming deadline. Sometimes cuddles are overshadowed by conference calls, and "quiet time" becomes a strategic game to try to ensure that Zoom meetings happen uninterrupted.

Being born during the pandemic meant that, for the first two years of his life, my son thought human interaction only occurred via a screen. His first birthday party was even held on Zoom, with everyone watching his first curious bite of cake from their respective sofas. As he grew, he became quite the little expert at quietly playing by himself while I talked to clients and recorded podcast episodes. And, though my meetings were never all that long and it certainly made things easier to have him adapt so well, I have to admit that even now I still feel the noxious presence of shame. Each and every time I peeked over my screen at him playing quietly with his cars, I'd feel a stab of guilt. (As we've established, the roots of mom guilt run deep.)

The reality is, though, that I am my son's primary financial provider. My businesses allow me to keep a roof over our heads, food on the table, and a steady stream of new Hot Wheels joining his garage. They also give me the freedom to be able to take him to the beach in the middle of the day and cuddle with him on the sofa when he's feeling icky. Having done my stint in the corporate world, I know full well that my businesses allow me to spend more time with him, even with my meetings, than I would if I were in a traditional nine-to-five.

Sometimes, being a mom means choosing the lesser of two evils. Maybe you don't love the idea of your kid zoning out on a tablet, but if it buys you a moment of peace to prevent a full-blown mental breakdown, then so be it. The truth is, that perfection in parenting is a myth. There's no way you can do everything right, all of the time. What is "right," anyways? It's a moving target, varying wildly from one mom to the next. For some, "right" may mean zero screen time. For others, it's letting their kid marathon-watch Bluey because that cheeky little blue dog brings them joy. The "right" choice is deeply personal, informed by your values, your child's needs, and a realistic assessment of the moment—along with as much guidance and awareness as possible for how kids develop physically, mentally, and spiritually.

Society sure has a lot to say about what it means to be a "good" mom, setting the bar higher than your secret stash of cookies you're trying to hide from your toddler. And, as much as it pains me to say it, *we* are often our worst enemies. I bet you are your own worst critic, pushing yourself to the brink, trying to be everything to everyone, and then beating yourself up when you inevitably can't meet your own impossible standards. Am I close?

Mom guilt has a way of crashing through the door like a toddler on a sugar high, especially for moms with businesses. It barges right in, demanding attention at the most inconvenient of times. Like at five am, when you're already knee-deep in emails, trying to catch that sliver of quiet work time before the house wakes up. Mom guilt is sitting right there with you, serving you up a side of "*Should I even be working right now?*" along with your coffee.

Or maybe it's at your back-to-back video calls, with your little one at the door, artwork in hand, eager to show you what they've made while you have to shush them quickly. Mom guilt rises up behind you, puts an arm gently around your shoulder, and smiles as it hisses in your ear, "A good mom would've found a way to do both."

Or maybe you're spending the afternoon outside, laughing and playing catch in the sunshine with your kids, all the while trying to dodge the feeling that you're slacking because you know you have an overflowing To-Do list awaiting your return. Perhaps it's fast food again for dinner because your day was a nonstop onslaught of fires to put out and you just didn't have the energy to cook. Would you like a biggie-sized helping of "*You should have planned better*" with that burger? And just when you've tucked your Littles into their beds and you sit down to take a moment for yourself and binge-watch your guilty pleasure, there's that nagging feeling again. *"Shouldn't you be doing something more productive?"* Mom guilt is with you throughout your entire day, ending ready to tuck you in sweetly with a bedtime story of doubt and "what ifs."

No matter the choice, mom guilt is there, ready with a one-way guilt-trip ticket. Choose work, and you're not spending enough time with your kids. Choose play, and you're slacking on your business goals. It's a lose-lose. It weaponizes your dreams and ambitions against you, suggesting that your pursuit of something beyond motherhood is selfish; that by following your passions and building something of your own, you're a bad mom and somehow failing your kids.

But here's a truth bomb for you: pursuing your passion, building your business, and providing for your family in every way possible (including financially) is not selfish—it's brave. It's powerful. It's part of what makes you an amazing mom. You're showing your kids the value of hard work, the importance of following your dreams, that success comes in many forms, and all the while teaching them about the balance and blend of family and personal fulfillment.

Being a mom with a business is not an either/or situation, it's a both/and. You're not taking away from your kids, you're adding to their lives by being a fulfilled, happy, whole person. Being a good mom isn't about meeting every expectation, whether it's your expectations, society's, or even the expectations you think your kids have. It's about showing up with unconditional love, ready to navigate this messy, beautiful chaos of raising tiny humans. It's about knowing that even on the days when you feel like you've got nothing left, you're still someone's everything. And mama, that is more than enough.

Though we typically label it mom "guilt," there's a crucial distinction to pay attention to here: guilt versus shame. Guilt says, "I did something bad." Shame says, "I *am* bad." Too often, we moms conflate the two, turning a moment of guilt into an indictment of our entire identity. Whatever we do, even if it's "right," we feel bad. But do you know what it means if you make a mistake? It simply means that you're a learning, living, growing human being. It doesn't mean you *are* a mistake. We have to consciously flip the script and refuse to let shame take root.

Because it becomes so linked to our identity, though, shame tends to be something that we don't often openly address. Ironically, there's a lot of shame about feeling shame. To tackle this head-on, you first have to be very open with yourself about who you are—what is your identity?

To answer this, look at what you value. What is important to you? *Who* is important to you? Why do you do whatever it is that you do? What are you passionate about, that thing that gets you up in the morning and makes you shine? From there, you can have an honest conversation with yourself about what is actually causing your guilt. Is it something that you really did do wrong? Is it an instance where you went against your values and compromised your convictions?

According to Merriam-Webster, "guilt" can refer to the state of having done something wrong, especially something that is punishable by law, or the *feeling* (that's key there) of responsibility for wrongdoing. If you did do something wrong (because let's be real, we all mess up every now and then), ask yourself how you can change the behavior and then, most importantly, *give yourself permission to move forward*. There's no point in beating yourself up nonstop for things that have already passed that you can't go back and change.

Sometimes guilt is an appropriate feeling, and could even be considered healthy. (Yep, I just said there's healthy guilt!) Our emotions don't exist just to keep things interesting—they're there to send a message. Sometimes guilt represents cognitive dissonance that sets in when we go against something we value or believe in, or if we violate a boundary we've set for ourselves. Healthy guilt helps you identify where that sneaky dissonance is—where you're acting against your blueprint, so to speak.

We all have a blueprint of who we think we are, the kinds of things we do or don't do, what we believe in, and even what we're capable of. If your actions don't match what you believe about yourself—if they don't match your blueprint of who you think you are—then cognitive dissonance and guilt will set in. When you feel this guilt, you then get to evaluate and decide whether you need to change your behavior or re-evaluate your blueprint.

For example, I worked with a woman who was plagued with guilt because she only worked on her business ten hours a week. When we dug deeper into her guilt, she was able to see that she didn't actually feel bad about the amount of time she worked. It was the *perfect* amount for her schedule, and let her spend time with her kiddos and take care of her mom. She only felt guilty because she *believed* she was supposed to work more than that. Someone had once taught her that if you worked less than forty hours a week, you weren't really working hard, and that belief got written into her blueprint. So her guilt was a sign that it was time to re-evaluate what she really believed and change her blueprint.

Toxic guilt, however, is another story. Mom guilt is usually toxic guilt. It's a feeling of shame even when you haven't done anything wrong.

In navigating guilt and shame, or healthy guilt and toxic guilt, the aim is not to harden ourselves against vulnerability but to have the guts to actually lean into it. It's in this space—the heart of vulnerability—that we find our most authentic selves, where we can distinguish between guilt that teaches and shame that wounds. Remember, vulnerability is not the enemy, it's the path through which we rediscover our worth and reaffirm our boundaries, rooted in our deepest values and truths.

Take Action

1. ***Calm your body.*** Guilt has a remarkable way of disrupting our nervous system and putting us in a panic state. Ground yourself, focus on your senses, take a few deep breaths, and even physically remove yourself from the situation if you can.
2. ***Check the facts.*** Do the facts support your feelings? Is this a feeling of healthy guilt that is trying to tell you something, or is this toxic guilt that needs to be called out and squashed right there and then?

   If what you're feeling is more akin to toxic guilt, ask yourself what you would tell your child if they came to you with the same feeling. What would you tell your friend? As I pointed out before, we're often our own harshest critics; where we would usually show others loving support and grace, we tend to stick to scathing reviews for ourselves.
3. ***Focus on self-awareness.*** Now that you're aware of the feeling, what are you going to do about it? If you feel guilt, it's an indication that you're attached to that particular value system. Is that a value you want to have? Or is it a value that someone else—your friends, your family, society, that "perfect" mom you follow on Instagram—has instilled in you that needs to be shifted?
4. ***Apologize.*** If your guilt is caused by something you did that maybe you shouldn't have, then the next step is to apologize to those involved. That could be your kids or other people, but it could also be

yourself. A lot of guilt is caused by us breaking our promises to ourselves. Like promising yourself that you're going to get up early to work out, only to hit snooze. Or promising that you're going to definitely, absolutely, without an ounce of doubt make progress on that project today, only to find yourself an hour later lost down a social media black hole. Recognize where you broke your promise, apologize, and move forward.

5. ***Create (or re-create) your boundaries.*** As we discussed earlier, feelings of guilt could come about if you find yourself making decisions that go against your identity, or, in other words, your personal blueprint for who you are and what you believe in. If you find yourself repeatedly in a state of cognitive dissonance, it's time to take a closer look at your boundaries. Is there a new boundary that needs to be put in place? Or maybe an existing boundary that needs to be re-evaluated?

You can best sustain your own boundaries if they are based on your own values. If you try to live based on someone else's blueprint, you'll repeatedly run into hardships. It won't feel true to you, you will fail, and you will feel guilt.

As you examine your blueprint, it's important not to label yourself. Whatever you declare yourself as becomes part of your identity—and becomes that much harder to change. For example, if you are a diehard fan of your local sports team and you suddenly show up to the next game wearing their rival's colors, well, the people who know you will call you out on it. Now, that's a bit of a simplified example, but the reality is that you subconsciously label yourself on a daily basis. Be aware of what labels you're using.

Instead of saying *I'm so busy*, acknowledge that it's a busy time right now.

Instead of saying *I'm lazy*, embrace that you're taking a well-deserved break and focusing on balance.

Instead of saying *I'm a bad mom*, know that you are doing your absolute best to provide a good life for your kids.

So, if you're one of the thousands upon thousands of moms out there feeling like they're not enough, remember this: you are more than enough. Every day, you show up, you love, you give, and that makes you not just a good mom but an incredible one. Let's toss out the lie of "I'm a bad mom" and replace it with the truth: "I'm the perfect mom for my kids and I am kicking butt at doing my absolute best."

3
I Should Be Further Along by Now

One of my favorite quotes, which has been a guiding light on my journey, is from Meera Lee Patel's beautifully illustrated book, *My Friend Fear*:

> *"Freedom is the recognition that where you are now is EXACTLY where you are supposed to be."*

That quote found its way to me when I was a fresh new mom, trying to navigate the demands of working a full-time job from home while trying to grow my business in the precious few hours my son napped each day.

Naptime became a sacred time in my household, and heaven help you if you were a door-to-door salesman who rang my doorbell and woke the baby up. I started to develop anxiety around naptime—*What if Greyson didn't sleep as usual? What if he woke up during my crucial client call? What if the dog decided that was the perfect time to bark?* What if, what if, what if.

I watched other entrepreneurs seemingly skyrocket to success, achieving milestones that felt light-years away from my reality. There they were, hitting six-figure months, publishing books, and landing speaking engagements. Meanwhile, I sat at my desk, sporting breastmilk stains and under-eye circles, desperately trying to get *something* done during my limited work time when all I wanted to do was curl up and sleep while the baby slept.

I was so fixated on the idea that *I should be further along than this*, that I completely lost sight of where I actually was: a new, single mom, navigating the steep learning curve of parenthood on my own during a global pandemic. It was time I gave myself credit for the monumental task I was managing and recognized that I was exactly where I needed to be. This was not just my reality but my moment to embrace the chaos, learn from it, and grow—not despite it, but because of it.

Picture this: It's late at night. The kids are finally asleep, and you've collapsed onto the couch. You pour yourself a mug of tea (or maybe a glass of wine—mama's choice) and for the first time today, it feels like you can breathe. You pull out your phone and scroll through social media, just needing a moment to unwind. Then you see it—a post from someone in one of your business groups, celebrating a big win, a goal that's also on your list.

Now, be honest with yourself—what's your initial reaction? I've posed this question to countless women I've coached over the years, and here are some of the most common emotions they've confessed:

Sadness.

Anger.

Jealousy.

Happy for her, but sad for me.

Feeling like things can work out for everyone else, but not for me.

Frustration.

There's something wrong with me.

I need to work harder.

I shouldn't be on social, I should be working instead.

Why can't I do that?

Impatience.

I should be further along by now.

That last one, "I should be further along by now," is an especially insidious little lie. It may seem like a fleeting notion at first, but it can grow to cast a shadow of doubt that then seeps into every single nook and cranny of your life, both personal and professional. It doesn't just question your business progress, it questions your effectiveness as a mother, partner, and friend. It digs its claws in deep, not just challenging your progress but making you question your entire journey—why aren't you where you think you should be? Why does it seem so much easier for everyone else? It's a narrative that, if left unchecked, can diminish your joy and cloud your vision.

I remember being a pre-teen, sprawled on the coarse gray carpet of Barnes and Noble, the smell of the in-store Starbucks making me feel very grown up (even though I didn't and still don't like coffee) as I flipped eagerly through stacks of glossy magazines. I was trying to get a peg on where exactly I was supposed to be in life and what I needed to do to get there. Ok, *Cosmo*, you're saying I should already have a boyfriend by now? I need to be married and pregnant before I turn twenty-five, got it. And, Martha, you're saying that to be a good homeowner, I need to learn how to embroider my own decorative pillowcases and bake all my own bread?

This barrage of expectations hasn't really changed over the years, it's only intensified with the rise of social media, where success stories and highlight reels are on loop 24/7. We live in a world that worships at the altar of achievement, where your worth is often measured by your latest accomplishment, and where we're constantly bombarded with tales of prodigies and entrepreneurs who skyrocketed to success overnight. The lie tells us that if we're not keeping up, we're falling behind, like being on a treadmill that keeps speeding up. No matter how fast you run, you'll never be able to catch up (you just feel sillier and sweatier as you scramble to try).

It can be easy to get swept up in stories or ads that boast about how someone "Gained one hundred new clients overnight! ... Went from broke to a seven-figure business! ... [Insert your own unrealistic but extremely tempting fantasy here.]" As a mom with a business, it's safe to say that you're ambitious and passionate, so it makes all the sense in the world that you would want to reach your goals as quickly as possible.

As a side note, before I continue, there are true rags-to-riches stories out there and people who have accomplished amazing things in their businesses in a short amount of time. I've had the honor of working with some amazing women over the years and have witnessed these transformations firsthand. But what you're not seeing are the countless hours spent toiling towards that goal, or the hundreds of little decisions that led to hundreds of small steps that added up, one after the other, to finally being able to accomplish the miraculous. To the outside person looking in, it may look like an "overnight" success. But to them, it's the culmination of a lifetime of work.

Social media, for all its benefits (and I do believe there are some benefits), often acts as a megaphone for this lie. We scroll through feeds filled with polished posts that are specifically curated to showcase only the peaks without the valleys. We often see snapshots of success without the backstory of all the struggles, failures, and the sheer grind it took to get there. This skewed portrayal creates a distorted benchmark of where we "should" be, igniting feelings of inadequacy and propelling the lie even further. In other words, you may be comparing Chapter 3 in your story to someone else's Chapter 23.

Here's the truth: life does not stick to a preset timeline. Milestones aren't one-size-fits-all. The pains of real progress are felt deeply and personally but are often invisible to the outside world. Growing pains aren't usually felt by anyone but the person doing the growing.

A few months ago, I was chatting with a friend who mentioned that both of her kids were reading by the time they were four. I nodded along in agreement like I was in the same boat with my son, all the while thinking to myself that I was failing as a teacher—Greyson, who was turning four at the end of the month, only knew his letter sounds and some sight words. No lie, I actually started thinking through lesson plans and how I could fit in a frenzied power study sesh to teach Greyson how to read fully by the end of the month. Luckily, that thought was fleeting and I instantly realized how completely and utterly ridiculous that need was.

When you're a mom with a business, I know firsthand how frustrating it can feel to know where you want to go and to see others getting to the destination ahead of you, but not have the time, energy, or mental bandwidth (or all of the above!) to make it happen at the same speed for yourself. I have been in seasons when it seems that I either have the desire to work towards my goals but lack the time, or I have time to work but feel too mentally and emotionally drained to do much of anything. It can be a rare day indeed when I get a big chunk of time to work and actually feel like I'm in a good headspace to get things done.

Try to remember that you are not defined by your pace or your progress. Your value doesn't diminish because your journey has detours or delays. In this vast world of entrepreneurship and motherhood, there is no set timeline, no universal benchmarks that you absolutely must hit. There's no "one way" to succeed in business (which we'll get into later on). There's only your path, your dreams, your pace, and that is enough.

I believe that self-respect is the primary language of self-love. A lot of people make the mistake of thinking they'll earn respect when they "make it" and have success. But self-respect isn't about impressing others quickly, it's about impressing yourself slowly, by taking one baby step after another, learning and growing, and developing a trusting relationship with yourself as you go. Self-respect doesn't come from being perfect, it comes from making progress.

Your journey is yours alone. It's unique, with its own set of challenges, victories, and lessons. Comparing your journey to someone else's is like comparing apples to spaceships—not only are they entirely different, but there's also no reason to compare in the first place. Remember, every entrepreneur, every mom, every person you admire and compare yourself to has faced their own struggles and setbacks throughout their journeys. What you're seeing is most likely the highlight reel. What you don't see are the sleepless nights, the self-doubt, the moments of failure that are universal to each and every one of us.

When our babies take their first precarious little steps, we cheer them on. We celebrate them, grabbing for our cameras with tears in our eyes and the biggest of smiles on our faces. We certainly don't chastise them for not being able to run yet. You have to learn how to walk before you can run. It's a progression—where you are right now is preparing you for the next step.

So, when that lie creeps in—"I should be further along by now"—challenge it. Demand of it, "Says who?" Break it down. Are you feeling this way because of societal pressures, or is it coming from a place of genuine desire for growth? If it's the latter, use it as fuel. Set small, achievable goals that will move you forward, step by step. Celebrate every win, no matter how small, because progress is progress.

But if the pressure is external, let's do some reprogramming. Affirm to yourself that you are exactly where you need to be. Your worth is not measured by your productivity, by whether you have hand-embroidered pillowcases or not, or by your business's revenue. You are not behind. You are on your own path, moving at your own pace, and that is more than okay. Society's (or anyone else's) script is not one you're obligated to follow. The great thing about your story is that *you're* the author; you can choose to reject external pressures and define success on your own terms. It's about rewriting the narrative to celebrate progress, not perfection, to value the journey as much as the destination, and to recognize that being "further along" is not a destination but a perpetual state of growth.

Take Action

1. ***Recognize your own timeline.*** Embrace that everyone's journey is different. Your business growth and your personal growth are not a race. (Say that again to yourself, if needed!) What works for one person in one year might take someone else three years...and that's okay! The first step to overcoming this lie is to accept that your timeline is yours alone, and it's perfectly tailored to your circumstances.
2. ***Celebrate the small wins.*** Often, we overlook the small successes because we're too focused on the big achievements. Start acknowledging, celebrating, and practicing gratitude for every single little win along the way. Whether it's a positive customer review, a small increase in sales, or heck, even just a day where you managed to shower and keep everyone fed, these are all significant. Celebrating these can provide a source of motivation and remind you that progress is still being made, even if it's just baby steps.
3. ***Set realistic goals.*** I'm all about dreaming big, but instead of setting monumental goals that are daunting and far-reaching, break them down into smaller, achievable targets. This will help make the journey a bit less overwhelming and will help you maintain a steady pace without burning out. You'll be able to measure your progress and celebrate those small wins along the way.
4. ***Reflect on your progress.*** I know they say don't look down... but look down. See how far you've

climbed. Battle those feelings of stagnation by creating a visual timeline of your achievements and challenges. Keep a journal of your progress so you can see the bigger picture of your growth.

5. ***Watch for social media comparisonitis.*** Social media can be a fantastic tool for networking, marketing, and bringing people together. It can also be a source of stress and unrealistic comparisons. Be intentional about how and when you use social media. Follow and engage with those who inspire you and make you feel good about your journey, rather than those who fuel comparison and doubt.
6. ***Reassess and adjust.*** It's okay to change your goals or your direction as you grow and learn more about your business and yourself. What seemed like a destination originally might just be a stepping stone to something else. Be flexible and open to adjusting your plans based on what's working...and what isn't.

And, if you need a little reminder and a bit of a pep talk, don't forget that the very act of balancing motherhood with entrepreneurship is a monumental achievement in and of itself. So, the next time you start to think, "I should be further along by now," remember: you're exactly where you're supposed to be. Your journey, with its ups and downs, its twists and turns, is beautiful, valid, and worth celebrating. Let go of where you think you "should" be and embrace where you are. Because, let me tell you, where you are right now is nothing short of remarkable.

4
What If I Fail?

Alright, it's confession time.

We're about to dive into the lie that was my own personal Mount Everest. Every single night, sometime around two am, you could find me lying awake in bed, the shadows on the ceiling dancing like specters of doubt, my mind actively being consumed by a whirlwind of worry, anxiety, and fear.

The thoughts would spiral out of control. Who did I think I was, trying to pull this off? I can't possibly do this. I'm going to fail. How will I ever support my family? What will people think? *Everyone will know I failed.*

I'd toss and turn, haunted by these intrusive thoughts, unable to escape the gripping fear that settled in the pit of my stomach. And the truly devastating part? I know I'm not the only one. In fact, I have yet to meet anyone who hasn't wrestled with a fear of failure at some point in their lives. Imagine that—all of us, lying awake in the dead of night, feeling utterly alone despite being in such vast company.

Failure is an all-too-common fear. It looms larger than life for most of us not just because of its immediate implications—missing the mark or not living up to expectations—but because of how deeply it's intertwined with our primal instincts. You see, our brains are hardwired for survival, an evolutionary trait designed to protect us from threats, like really big things with sharp teeth that wanted to eat us. Incredibly useful ages ago, but today? It's this same instinct that sends us into a spiral of anxiety over modern "threats" such as launching a new product, making a significant career shift, or even just posting on social media.

It also doesn't help that we're conditioned to value success as the ultimate of ultimate benchmarks, painting failure not just as a setback, but as a personal weakness; that failure is a stain on our character. This creates a vicious cycle where we tie our self-worth directly to our achievements—and, painfully, to our failures.

One could also argue that perfectionism—in itself a self-destructive and addictive belief system—is directly tied to our fear of failure. Perfectionism tricks us into believing that if something isn't flawless, it's not worth doing at all. Think about it: if you never actually finish that project, if it's eternally "in progress," never quite ready for the spotlight, then *technically* you can't fail, right? This mindset might shield you from potential failures, but it also holds you back from all the amazing things you could get from growth and success.

I had a mentor who used to say repeatedly, "You can't win if you don't play the game." (And I would repeatedly roll my eyes at how cheesy and utterly clichéd the platitude was...) But the core message is undeniably true, and it resonates deeply, especially as an entrepreneur. Here's the raw truth: If you never take that leap to start your business, you'll remain on the sidelines, watching others play the game you want to be in. If you hold back your new product because it's not "perfect" yet, it will never get a chance to dazzle your audience or change someone's world the way you dreamed it could. If you never try, if you never even put yourself out there, success will always be a distant and untouchable goal.

The reality is, that stepping into the arena (or field, or diamond, or court, or whatever the proper sports analogy is) is where the magic happens. It's about embracing the mess, the uncertainty, and even the potential for failure because *that's where the growth lives*. It's about understanding that every giant achievement starts with the decision to try, to play, to participate fully in your own dreams.

In day-to-day life, the fear of failure can manifest in many different ways. Sometimes it's a blatant, stare-you-directly-in-the-face type of fear like those two am Dread Fests. Other times, it shows up in more subtle (but nonetheless impactful) ways that undermine your actions and decisions.

Think about the moment right before you hit "send" on a new marketing email. There's a hesitation, an inkling of doubt about how it will be received. Or it's that pause before you share your latest post, as that sneaky little thought creeps in that no one is going to like it—and then everyone will see that no one likes it. It's the same lie that holds you back from reaching out to potential collaborators or clients because you're scared of being rejected, or worse, not taken seriously.

To be frank, fear of failure can often lead to pulling your punches. Instead of your wild and big goals, maybe you'll shift your sights lower to a smaller target that feels safer and easier to hit. It may mean choosing not to invest in that business coach or that new bit of software that could take your business to the next level because you're worried about the financial what-ifs.

This lie doesn't just stunt your business's growth, it can lead to personal burnout, too. Driven by the dread of failing, you might take on too much, agree to every request that comes your way, and push yourself to (and sometimes past) the brink of exhaustion. When you most need a break to recharge and refocus, fear compels you to keep on grinding. You end up sacrificing time with your family and friends, your health, and your overall well-being, all because you're driven by a fear of what might happen if you don't.

Emotionally, constantly asking yourself, "What if I fail?" lays a heavy burden on your shoulders. The weight of it (and the anxiety and stress that naturally come with it) can cloud your judgment, block your intuition, and dampen your creativity. It's hard to innovate and take well-calculated risks when you're continually weighed down by worry. Ultimately, this fear can and will strip the joy from your work, turning the passion that used to fuel you and add that little pep to your step into a series of anxiety-inducing tasks that you dread.

When I was a kid, I loved the *Goosebumps* books and TV show. One episode that I found particularly terrifying was "It Came from Beneath the Sink," in which there was an evil sponge that made all sorts of bad things happen. (Okay, so that sounds a little anticlimactic now when I write it like that, but as a kid, I swear it was terrifying!) Spoiler alert, the killer sponge fed off all the negativity. The only way to destroy it was to shower it with love and kindness. In order to move past this fear of failure, you have to do something counterintuitive: You have to get cozy with it.

The secret is not to run from your fear but to embrace it, hug it tight, and maybe even pinch its cute little cheeks a bit. When you're lying in bed, your heart racing and your mind whirling with all of the "what ifs" and doomsday scenarios, it's easy to view fear as the enemy. It may be hard to believe, but that fear niggling at you in the quiet hours of the night isn't actually the bad guy. It's not a killer sponge feeding off your dread and anxiety. It isn't the villain of your story. It's more like the quirky sidekick that's just a bit overzealous at doing its job.

The reality is, that fear is actually one of your greatest allies; it's trying to protect you. Fear's real role is to try to keep you safe and to shield you from pain and loss. But in doing so, it sometimes gets a wee bit overprotective and can hold you back from taking the leaps that lead to growth, joy, and success. And, if you listen, it's sharing secrets about what truly matters to you.

Think about it—fear doesn't show up unless there's something on the line, something important and valuable to you. Whether it's that unique nerve-wracking feeling of starting your own business, stepping onto a stage in front of a crowd to speak, or publishing your first book, fear is there because you care. Deeply. That heart-pounding, palm-sweating, toss-your-cookies-inducing sensation is a signal, pointing you toward your passions and the things in life that hold the deepest meaning for you. It's fear's way of whispering, "Hey, this matters."

What if instead of pushing that fear away, you leaned into it? What if you listened to what it's trying to tell you? For instance, the fear of launching a new product isn't just about the risk of it flopping. It's terrifying because every detail of your product reflects your vision, your sweat (and maybe even some tears), and your late nights and early mornings. There's a vulnerability in this process, a piece of your own story and identity embedded in this new product. And so, the fear of failure becomes deeply personal. It's not simply a matter of market dynamics or consumer preferences. If they don't buy, it feels like they're not just rejecting the product—you feel like they're rejecting *you*.

So how do you turn this frenemy into a friend? Start by asking it, "What are you trying to protect me from?"

and listen to the answer. Maybe it's safeguarding you from financial trouble, embarrassment, or the thought of having all your old high school friends on your social see you struggling. (Seriously, be honest, have you ever stopped yourself from posting something because you were worried about what your Aunt Rachel or so-and-so from third-period Geometry would think? I'll admit that I've absolutely had those thoughts over the years.) Recognize that your fear's intentions are good—it's more of a guard dog than a monster out to get you.

Next, reassure your fear. Let it know that you appreciate its vigilance, but you've got this. Show how you're prepared to handle the risks it's so worried about. Draw up plans, build safety nets, and get your strategies in place. Think about what could go wrong—not so that you can manifest it, but so you can have a plan in place and (in most cases) see that it's really not as bad as all that. And then think about what could go *right*.

It's time to gently but firmly remind your fear who's boss. You are in charge of your life, not your fear. Acknowledge its presence but don't let it take control. Focus on what's real right now— and even if you do fail, it's not the end. Failure is just the beginning. It's a lesson learned (granted, sometimes they're really hard lessons...), but it is still just feedback. Each failure carries a nugget of wisdom that you can use to move forward with more clarity and determination—or you can decide to give up completely. You have the power to choose how you respond to failure. You can let it be the end, or you can let it be the beginning of something greater. You can wallow in self-pity, or you can dust yourself off and say, "Okay, what's next?" The choice is yours.

Embrace an experimental mindset and ask yourself, "How can I make this better?" Normalize failure, and learn to talk about and celebrate your failures as much as you celebrate your successes. This transparency changes the narrative that to fail is to lose *into* to fail is to learn.

Is it really true that everyone will think less of you if you fail? Probably not. Lean into the discomfort. Acknowledge your fear of failure, sit with it, understand it, and then move through it. Avoiding your fear only amplifies it. Use your fear as a compass to guide you toward what really matters, what's worth fighting for, and what deserves your energy.

Finally, channel that fear into fuel. Every entrepreneur, leader, parent, and successful person in the history of ever has faced fear head-on and used it to propel themselves forward. They've embraced the butterflies, used the adrenaline, and allowed fear to push them out of their comfort zones and into their potential. Facing the fear of failure isn't about eradicating it, it's about moving forward despite it being by your side. It's about choosing courage over comfort, practicing our values rather than simply professing them, and recognizing that failure is not a final destination, but a stepping stone to success.

Take Action

1. ***Own your story.*** Own every single part of your journey, especially the failures. When I first started my business, I had more "failures" than successes. Ads that tanked, projects that I lost money on because I undercharged, courses that I invested in that I never finished, ideas that flopped spectacularly. But each of those failures taught me something vital about how to succeed the next time. I would like to encourage you to share your struggles openly. When you own your story, your failures become more like badges of honor—signs of the growth you've had to go through and the progress you've made—than anything else.
2. ***Analyze and adapt.*** After each setback, take a deep breath and then dive into what went wrong. Were there warning signs? Did you veer away from your core values or strengths? Was it something outside of your control? Or maybe it was an example of a time when you just didn't know what you didn't know, and now you know. Analyzing your failures helps you adapt. Maybe you need to pivot your approach, learn a new skill, or just find a little grit and dig in and try again. Remember, clarity often comes from action, not thought.
3. ***Reset your goals.*** Sometimes failure means that your goals need reshaping. Perhaps they were too vague, too ambitious for where you were at the time, or maybe not ambitious enough. Set new, clear, actionable goals based on what you've learned. Now, this doesn't mean lowering your standards—it

means setting smarter, sharper targets that propel you forward.

4. ***Cultivate resilience.*** Resilience isn't about never feeling that sting of defeat, it's about learning how quickly you can stand up after a fall. Develop daily habits that help strengthen your mental and emotional resilience. Write affirmations, practice gratitude, listen to a motivational podcast while you're brushing your teeth—feed your spirit with positivity and watch how it transforms your attitude towards failure.
5. ***Keep on keeping on.*** The key to overcoming failure is not stopping. Failure is only the end if you don't keep moving forward. Take at least one action, even if it's a baby step, towards your dreams every single day. No matter how small it may seem, progress is progress. As long as you're moving, you're on your way to something great.

Remember, that road to success is pretty much almost never a straight line. It's a winding path with highs and lows and potholes and breaks for naps and snacks and dropped toys you have to double back to find. But each step, even the missteps, is moving you forward. Embrace them, learn from them, and keep pushing forward.

5
There's Only One Right Way to Do This

I'm a massive advocate for betting on yourself by investing in tools that foster growth. Whether it's a coach who can offer guidance, a course that teaches you new skills, a membership that surrounds you with go-getters, or any other resource that pushes your boundaries—these investments can be game-changers. Over the years, as I've built my businesses, I've made it a point to pour into my personal development. And let me tell you, most of these investments have paid off immensely, catapulting me to levels of success I once only dreamed about.

But let's be real. There were also quite a few programs I invested in that I didn't fully engage with—or even complete.

Don't get me wrong, they were great resources. Understanding the strategies? No problem. Appreciating their value? Absolutely. But when it came to implementing these strategies? That's where the struggle hit. My schedule was essentially a three-ring circus—juggling a full-time job, working with my own clients, and raising my little one left practically no room to actually put what they were teaching into practice. I didn't have the bandwidth to post multiple times a day on social media, attend endless networking events, email my list daily, or whip up a course over a weekend.

Plus, to be honest, some of the strategies just didn't align with my strengths or what I envisioned for my business. (I have come to accept that small talk in the DMs just isn't my thing.) And then there were the occasional teachings that actually clashed with my core values (like telling potential clients that they should get a second mortgage or tap into their 401k to pay for my offers). That's a hard pass for me.

In one mentorship program in particular, the coach instructed us to block off four hours daily for three weeks to dive deep into her training. I had a major reality check—my son had just figured out how to crawl and keeping him from wreaking havoc (and terrorizing the cats) was practically a full-time gig in itself. Four hours? I was lucky to snag four uninterrupted minutes! During a group call, I confessed my struggle with the schedule and asked for help pivoting the strategies a bit to fit my lifestyle better. The coach's rather blunt response was that I would never succeed in business unless I did things her way.

I'll admit that it stung, watching the other students in the program seemingly effortlessly skyrocket to success using the same tools that were gathering digital dust on my computer. I felt like there was something wrong with me, that I just couldn't make things work. It felt like I was doomed to fail because I couldn't stick to the "proven" path everyone else was cruising along.

But success isn't one-size-fits-all. And neither is the path to get there. I learned the hard way that it's about finding what works for you, playing to your strengths, and staying true to your values. And sometimes, that means walking away from a coach or strategy that doesn't align with *your* life's reality.

Our brains sure do love a shortcut. Especially our overwhelmed, exhausted, trying-to-do-a-million-things-at-once business mom brains. Our brains crave simplicity and a clear, straightforward, easy-to-follow path. It's why we're so tempted by the diet that promises quick results by cutting out *this one thing* or the business strategy that guarantees success if you just follow *these ten simple steps*. Our brains are hardwired to seek out patterns and shortcuts, making the allure of a "proven" method that much harder to resist.

It's also super scary to step out into the unknown. We already know that the fear of making a mistake or failing can paralyze even the best of us. When someone hands you a roadmap and says, "Hey, this worked for me, it will work for you," it's comforting. It feels safer to walk a well-trodden path than to hack through the underbrush, not knowing what you'll find.

There's also the fact that we're ultimately social beings (yes, even the most introverted of us). We look around, see what others are doing, and naturally, we think, "If it worked for them, that must be the way for me, too." Whether it's the pressure from seeing perfectly curated lives on social media or even just hearing that other mom at the park swear by her morning routine, the pressure to conform is real. It makes us believe that if we step outside of these norms, we're doomed to fail. That there is only one way to succeed.

As an entrepreneur, the myth that there's only one way to succeed (and, spoiler alert, it *is* a myth) can be especially stifling. Think about it. How many times have you held back from trying a new approach because it wasn't the industry standard? How often have you compared your chapter one to someone else's chapter twenty because they followed "The Formula"? This lie can trap you in a cycle of comparison and missed opportunities, ultimately smothering the spark of innovation and strangling your intuition because you're too afraid to venture off the prescribed path.

In parenting, this myth can also make you feel like you're constantly failing (hello mom guilt, my old friend) because you're not doing it the way that bestselling book or that influencer says you should. In the daily grind of managing a business and a family, this lie manifests in the choices that you make about how to allocate your time, how to manage your responsibilities, and how you prioritize your goals. Maybe you've felt the pressure to follow parenting methods that just don't fit your family's dynamic. Or perhaps you've been told there's only one way to balance work and home life, and it leaves you feeling less than inadequate when it doesn't pan out for you. This myth can make you second-guess every decision, from how you handle toddler tantrums to how you launch your next product.

First things first, the idea that there's a singular path to success in business or a cookie-cutter approach to parenting just isn't true. We all come from diverse backgrounds, we all have different strengths and weaknesses, and—let's be real—what works for one person might be a total disaster for another.

In the world of business, especially as a mom, flexibility and adaptability are your best friends. Some may tell you that you have to get up at four am and knock out a couple of hours of work before the rest of the household rises. But if you just spent half the night up with a sick child, that model isn't going to be your friend. Not in the least.

Maybe you choose to put your kids in childcare during the day.

Maybe you don't.

Maybe you choose to homeschool and work while the kids are going through their lessons.

Maybe you don't.

Maybe you choose to play all day with your kids and then fit in a full workday after they go to bed.

Maybe you don't.

Success in your business comes from creating a schedule that fits your life, not squeezing your life into someone else's schedule. The "right way" is the way that works for you, generates revenue, and keeps you passionate about what you're doing.

As for parenting, that same rule applies. One-size-fits-all parenting advice? Toss it out. Whether it's co-sleeping, homeschooling, screen time, or any of the hot debate topics—what works best for one family might be impractical or impossible for another. You know your children best. Trust your instincts, and tailor your parenting time to fit each child's needs and your family values.

And guess what? The same concept applies to marketing strategies. I can't count the number of times someone has come to me for help, feeling overwhelmed and discouraged because they don't like being on social media, and that's the "only way" to grow a business. Or they don't have time to create videos. Or they don't want to send cold messages to people. Here's the truth: You don't have to. It's not the only way.

Now, don't get me wrong. There are some things you're going to have to do in business (and in life) that you just don't want to do. If you despise *all* forms of marketing and therefore refuse to do *anything*, well, that's not going to lead to a very healthy business.

But here's the thing: You are unique. Your magic combination of strengths, weaknesses, qualifications, values, and life experiences is exactly what will make your business stand out—not how well you can fit yourself into someone else's framework. Maybe you're a natural at creating engaging videos—a main pillar of your marketing strategy can be to make videos to attract new leads and nurture your existing ones. Or maybe you're a really good writer—focus on your blog, writing for magazines, or even writing a book. Your strengths are your superpowers, and they should guide your business and marketing strategies.

Learning from others, investing in new experiences, and growing your skill sets are all fantastic things. But the *only* way to truly succeed in business and grow something that fuels your passions is to understand that there *isn't* only one right way to be successful.

Start by identifying your unique strengths and passions. What sets you apart? What do you love doing? Lean into those aspects of yourself and let them shine in your business. Your authenticity will resonate with your audience and make your brand unforgettable. It's important to create business and marketing strategies that fit your life and your strengths. Don't be afraid to trust your instincts; you know your business and your audience better than anyone else. Trust your gut when it comes to making decisions. If something doesn't feel right or align with your values or fit with your lifestyle needs, don't do it. Not every tip or strategy will be right for you, *and that's okay*. Adapt what you learn to fit your unique situation.

Going back to the beginning of this chapter, at this stage in my journey, I have no problems finishing every program I commit to, and let me tell you, it's not because I've miraculously found more hours in the day! My little Greyson may not be that tiny, cat-chasing crawler anymore, but as he's grown, his needs have evolved, too. Every stage brings new adventures and challenges. What has changed, though, is how I choose where to invest my time and resources.

Now, I only put my energy and my dollars into programs led by people who walk their talk—those whose values resonate deeply with my own. I choose leaders who aren't just talking from high up on a pedestal, they're the ones who've been down in the hole, who've faced challenges similar to mine, and have come out the other side stronger. They're real, they're raw, and they understand the journey because they've lived it. Connecting with them and their teachings feels more authentic to me because it's grounded in shared experiences and mutual understanding. It's empowering to learn from someone who gets it—who understands that while I'm passionate about growing my business, I'm also a mom navigating the wilds of raising a tiny human.

While going your own way is vital, so is finding a supportive community. Connect with other moms who are in the trenches of motherhood and entrepreneurship. Sharing ideas and supporting each other can help you discover new, personalized ways of managing business and family life. These connections can affirm that while your methods might differ, the challenges you face are often similar. I have many supportive business friends who aren't moms and many supportive mom friends who aren't entrepreneurs. But, let me tell you, no one—and I mean no one—gets me and what I'm going through better than the other moms with businesses.

You will also need to embrace the fact that you will undoubtedly need to pivot numerous times. What worked last year might not work this year. Both your business and your children will grow and change, and so should your strategies. Stay open to learning, whether it's from books, podcasts, mentors, or your own mistakes.

Whether it's your business strategy or your parenting style, make it yours. Customize it to fit your strengths, your schedule, and your values. Experiment and iterate. Some of the most successful businesses and the most joyful parenting experiences come from forging your own path. The truth is, no one else can do it quite like you. No one else has your background, your history, or your unique mix of talents and strengths. Your unique perspective is what sets you apart, so lean into it. Embrace your journey, with all the beauty, chaos, and messiness it entails. Embrace courageous rejection of the idea that there's only one path to success.

Take Action

1. ***Identify what works for you.*** First things first, grab your journal and start listing out all the things about your business and parenting style that are currently working for you. Maybe it's your flexible work hours, or how you integrate family time into your daily routine. Recognizing what's already successful is your first step to undermining the "one way" myth.
2. ***Define your values.*** What are the core values that drive both your family life and your business? Write them down. This could be integrity, creativity, independence, service, or something else. Your path should align with these values, not with someone else's blueprint for success. Decisions become easier when you ask, "Does this align with my values?"
3. ***Seek diverse perspectives.*** Actively look for mentors and peers who break the mold. These might be other entrepreneurial moms who are also doing things their own way. Follow their blogs, listen to their podcasts, or join their communities. Seeing how others successfully navigate their unique challenges will inspire you to think differently about your own situation.
4. ***Experiment boldly.*** The best way to prove that multiple methods can lead to success is to try new approaches yourself. Experiment with different business strategies or parenting hacks and observe what works best for your unique family and business dynamic. Maybe it's a new marketing strategy, an

asynchronous sales method, or a new family routine. Innovation is your friend!

5. ***Reflect and adjust regularly.*** Take time to check in with what's working... and what isn't. Be honest with yourself during these reflections, and be willing to pivot without seeing it as a setback. This ongoing process allows you to refine your approach continually and adapt to whatever season you happen to be in with your business and personal life.

Remember, there is incredible power in paving your own way. When you stop trying to fit into someone else's idea of success, you open up a world where you can thrive on your own terms. I like to encourage all my clients to "take the chicken and leave the bones." (I actually find the visual of that mildly gross, but maybe that's why it sticks in my head!) It's a reminder to make decisions that truly reflect who you are and what you want to achieve. Choose business practices that play to your strengths, and parent in a way that feels good to you and meets your family's needs.

The next time you hear, "*This* is the only way to do this," smile because you know the truth. There's only one right way for you, and mama, you're already on it. Forge ahead, be bold, rewrite the rules. It's the only way to succeed in business.

6
Imperfect Equals Inadequate

The other day, Greyson decided he was going to make me a snack. “Mama, you just relax!” he chirped, that sweet little voice just bubbling with excitement. “I’ll get us a snack!” It was the sweetest thing.

Then came the moment of truth. Greyson, bless his heart, came slowly over toward me, his face lit up with pride, carrying a serving tray balancing glasses of water, fruit snacks, apples, and bowls of Goldfish crackers. Just as he reached me, it happened. The apples rolled and the drinks took a dive, clattering to the floor and splashing all over his legs. He stared at the mess, his lower lip quivering, and I tensed, expecting the tears to come flowing. But instead, he looked up at me, shrugged, laughed, and said, “Well, that’s one way to do it!”

I tell you what, I was one proud mama.

Watching Greyson that day he made snacks, in that perfectly imperfect moment, I realized something powerful. It's not about the mess or the mistakes—it's about the attempt, the effort, the joy found in simply giving it a go. Greyson wasn't worried about the spilled tray, he was just thrilled to be making mommy a snack. He found joy in the "doing" rather than the "perfecting."

I have no problem admitting that I spent most of my life as a card-carrying member of the perfectionist club. As a kid, I was a straight-A student. When I got my first house, I worked tirelessly to keep it so clean and organized that it could have doubled as a spread in *Better Homes and Gardens* (this was, of course, pre-children). As a business owner, I wouldn't dream of launching anything that wasn't absolutely flawless.

It was downright exhausting and equated to a bunch of missed opportunities. I often said no to friends dropping by because the house wasn't "ready." Countless business ideas gathered digital dust in my Google Drive because they weren't "just right" yet.

At the core, much of our drive for perfection stems from a deep-seated fear of being judged or rejected. We're social creatures, hardwired to seek acceptance and avoid rejection at all costs. Historically, being part of a group meant protection, resources, and survival. In our ancestral past, rejection from the group could lead to isolation and death. Fast forward to modern times, this need for belonging and fear of rejection still lingers. The stakes may not be as high, but our brains react similarly to social exclusion as they do to physical danger.

Perfectionism often gives us the illusion of control in an unpredictable world. If we can just perfect every single aspect of our lives, we believe we can control how others perceive us and, ultimately, control our own happiness and success. This illusion is powerful—but deeply flawed. Life is inherently unpredictable, and no amount of perfect planning can change that.

At its core, the lie "imperfect equals inadequate" abounds from a cocktail of perfectionism and comparisonitis. It's fed by societal expectations and is amplified by the highlight reels we stream on TV and scroll through on social media every day. We celebrate the wins and hide the struggles, which paints a skewed picture of reality. This cultural backdrop makes it oh-so-easy to equate imperfection with failure, especially for moms in the business world, where our professional and parental roles often collide spectacularly. But here's the truth—these expectations are not only unrealistic, they're unsustainable. Perfectionism is a relentless taskmaster, and it tricks us into believing that if we're not doing everything flawlessly, we're failing.

Perfectionism can also be seen as a coping mechanism to deal with uncertainty. In a world where so much is beyond our control, focusing on perfecting our actions and environments can give us some semblance of control. We might believe that if we can make everything perfect, we can prevent bad outcomes and ensure positive ones. However, this belief is flawed. No matter how much we plan, life is still inherently unpredictable. The weather changes, markets crash, drinks spill.

From a young age, we're bombarded with messages about what success looks like. Whether it's through the media, schooling, or parental expectations, we internalize a standard of "what should be." Often, we set our bar at this level without ever considering whether that bar is realistic or even what we truly want. As we know, these internalized expectations can turn into harsh self-criticism if we fail to meet them. (Which is inevitable.)

Think about the gold stars for perfect homework, the accolades for scoring the winning goal, the little paper certificates you get for high achievements in school. Perfection is praised. But let's get real—life isn't about a collection of perfect moments strung together. Achievements should be celebrated, absolutely, but so should the journey. It's not just about reaching the peak, it's about every single step you take to get there.

Here's the thing. Striving for growth and pushing your limits is vital. I'm all about continually pushing myself to new heights. My biggest role model? The person I'm going to be in five years. But let's celebrate that progress, appreciate the baby steps we take on the path to growth, and remember that every stumble and imperfection is part of that path.

Most of my perfectionism stemmed from the idea that I needed to "earn" or "prove" my worth. That's an exhausting cycle, suggesting our worth is conditional—something that can be gained or lost based on our achievements or failures. It implies that our value as individuals is tied to our performance rather than being inherent. This notion can lead to endless overworking, chronic stress, and an attitude of never being fully satisfied.

How does this show up in your life? Maybe it shows up as being overly critical of your parenting, your appearance, or going through relentless revisions of projects, never feeling fully satisfied with completed work. Do you find yourself redoing tasks that were already done well? Or maybe you hesitate to share work until it's "perfect," or avoid new challenges out of fear of not excelling. This endless pursuit of perfection can stifle creativity, as the fear of making mistakes can prevent you from trying new things.

One of the most powerful antidotes to perfectionism is self-compassion. Recognize that being human means being inherently imperfect. Vulnerability is not about weakness but about the courage to show up and be seen, imperfections and all.

Share your true self, your struggles, and your not-so-perfect moments. This will not only liberate you from the chains of perfectionism but allow others to connect with you more genuinely. Shift from a mindset of proving to *im*proving. Focus on growth and learning rather than perfect outcomes. Celebrate progress, not perfection, and remember that every misstep is a stepping stone to greater wisdom and strength.

Take a moment and think about who you love. Who are they to you? What are some of their character traits that you love? What are some of their character traits that you could, quite frankly, do without?

I don't love my son because he's perfect. I love him unconditionally, regardless of his flaws or faults, the fact that he kicks like crazy in his sleep, forgets to cover his mouth sometimes when he sneezes, or that he's going through a wicked potty talk phase at the moment. And I imagine that you're the same way. Those whom you love most likely aren't perfect. They have their own shortcomings and areas in which they can grow. But you love them, nonetheless.

It shouldn't be that big a stretch, then, for us to be able to love ourselves despite our imperfections. Real love isn't about honoring what's perfect, it's about embracing what's imperfect.

It's easy to see the little bumps in the road as giant roadblocks, but try to embrace hardships for what they are—opportunities to learn and to grow. Leaning into challenges expands who we are and helps strengthen our relationship with ourselves. When we're put through tough situations, we learn what we're made of, because we are at our absolute strongest only when strong is the last option we have.

That means that instead of being critical of yourself for not being perfect, look for ways to appreciate yourself, love yourself, honor yourself, and value yourself as much and as often as you can. You are worthy right now, exactly as you are, imperfections and all. Let go of the exhausting need to prove your worth through perfection. Instead, pour that energy into living authentically, loving fiercely, and leading courageously. Because you, just as you are, are enough.

Take Action

1. ***Own your story.*** Start by embracing this unique, amazing, wonderful (albeit sometimes chaotic) journey that you're on. Every struggle, every setback, and every win has shaped you into the incredible kick-booty-butt person you are today. Share your story with pride. When you own your imperfections, you take away their power to make you feel inadequate. Your authenticity is your strength—let it shine.
2. ***Redefine success.*** Success isn't about being flawless, it's about growth, resilience, and learning. Take a moment to write down what success truly means to you. Is it being able to spend quality time with your kiddos? Building a business that aligns with your values? Making enough to help your partner retire to pursue their passions? Making a positive impact in your community? Redefine success on your terms and let go of anyone else's standards.
3. ***Practice self-compassion.*** I'm using my mom voice now: Be nice. Specifically, to yourself. When you make a mistake or have to deal with a setback, talk to yourself like you would a friend or your child. Acknowledge your efforts and remind yourself that it's okay to be imperfect. Remember, self-compassion isn't about lowering your standards, it's about recognizing your worth regardless of your achievements.

4. ***Start with the MVP.*** I'm all about implementing the "minimum viable product" method when you're putting something new together. What is the minimum level something needs to be before you can launch it? If it's an offer, what's the bare minimum you need to make sure your clients find success with it? Launch your MVP, knowing that you can and will come back to it and take it to the next level. This allows you to focus on progress, not perfection. It also helps you get real-world feedback on your project.
5. ***Embrace flexibility.*** Life is unpredictable, especially when you're balancing a business and a family. Embrace flexibility and be willing to adapt. Perfectionism often stems from a desire to control everything, but real growth happens when you learn to go with the flow and adjust your plans as needed.
6. ***Focus on strengths, not weaknesses.*** Identify your strengths and leverage them. Instead of dwelling on what you can't do perfectly, focus on what you do exceptionally well. Use your strengths to your advantage.
7. ***Learn from imperfections.*** Each and every imperfection is an opportunity to learn and grow. When something doesn't go as planned (which I'm sure you know can happen a lot), reflect on what you can learn from that experience. This mindset shift turns setbacks into valuable lessons and helps you see imperfections as stepping stones to success.
8. ***Celebrate your wins.*** Big or small, celebrate your achievements. Take time to recognize your hard

work and dedication. Each win, no matter how minor it may seem, is a step towards your ultimate goal. Celebrating your successes keeps you motivated and reinforces a positive mindset.

9. ***Surround yourself with positivity.*** Who are the people in your life who love you unconditionally, flaws and all? Find your community of like-minded individuals who understand your journey because they're living it, too. Their encouragement and support will remind you that imperfection is just part of the process, and they can love you when maybe you're not as loving to yourself.
10. ***Let go of comparison.*** Mama, stop comparing your journey to others. Comparison is the thief of joy. Your path is your own. Use the progress of others to inspire you, and to motivate you to continue pushing, but celebrate your progress without measuring it against someone else's journey.

Imperfection doesn't equal inadequacy. Your imperfections make you real, relatable, and resilient. By embracing them, you not only free yourself from unrealistic standards and the stress that comes with them—you also inspire others to do the same. You are enough—powerful, capable, worthy—just as you are. Keep growing and being unapologetically you.

7
But That's Been Done Before

I love my mama. She's empathetic and caring and makes the best darn homemade ice cream you'll have just about anywhere. She's also an extraordinary artist. There's not a moment in my life when I can't remember her knee-deep in some sort of creative project. Whether she was sketching out illustrations for a children's book, painting a purple wisteria vine to bloom across my little sister's room, or expertly tucking a new plant into the lush flower beds that surrounded our home, she made sure we were always surrounded by beauty and creativity. I recall evenings spent at the kitchen table, her art supplies strewn about and the air thick with the smell of acrylics, as she patiently taught us how to blend with colored pencils.

Her journey in horticulture started almost half a century ago, at a small local garden center. Over the years, her passion bloomed into a full-fledged art form. She creates the most stunning container gardens you can imagine, a riot of colors and fragrances. She's won awards for her designs, people beg her to give talks about the art of container gardening, she's been featured in news articles, interviewed on TV and radio, and each spring there's a line out the door at the greenhouse where she works, with folks clamoring to buy one of her custom creations.

Despite all this, she doesn't see her own brilliance. Every time I suggest (like the serial entrepreneur I am) that she brands her creations, launches a custom line, or even starts a course to share her wealth of knowledge, she just shrugs it off. "Anyone can put together a container garden," she says. "This isn't unique. Other people do this."

Sound familiar? "But that's been done before!" is a classic entrepreneurial fear that has stopped so many dreams in their tracks. How many times have you had a brilliant idea but hesitated to pursue it because someone else had already done something similar?

Here's the truth: originality isn't about being the first to do something, it's about bringing your unique perspective and passion to the table. My mom's container gardens aren't just plants in pots—they're a reflection of her artistry, her care, and her love. And that is something no one else can replicate.

This lie often stems from a fear of redundancy. We worry that because something exists, there's no room for our version. We see the market as a finite pie instead of an expandable universe that shifts and grows with each new innovation. This is a scarcity mindset, where we believe that success for others means less opportunity for us.

Nowadays, it's easy to scroll through feeds filled with successes and think, "Well, that's it. I can't top that. Better close up shop." It's not just discouraging, it's downright debilitating. It can prevent you from even starting, paralyzing you with the idea that because you can't be first, maybe you shouldn't bother being anything at all.

Humans tend to have a deep-seated need to be seen and recognized—to feel like we matter. The fear behind "but that's been done before" is often a fear of invisibility. We worry that if we do something similar to what others have done, we won't stand out, and thus, we won't be seen. Or worse, we'll be seen and others will realize that we don't measure up. (Cue the deeper fears of inadequacy and irrelevance.)

This fear is also a perfect representation of cognitive bias, specifically the availability heuristic. (Whoa, what?) This fancy term is basically a mental shortcut our brains use to make quick judgments about a situation based on the information readily available. It's like trying to decide what's for dinner, and all you can think about is pizza because you just saw a pizza commercial. Our brains use the most immediate examples available to make decisions, which can sometimes lead us down a bit of a tricky path, especially when social media algorithms and tracking cookies come into play.

Let's say you run a blog for moms, sharing the latest parenting hack or must-have product for your kid. Now imagine you're scrolling through Instagram trying to find inspiration for your next blog. The algorithm already knows what kinds of topics interest you, so inevitably you'll end up seeing other successful bloggers just like you. Each swipe up leads to more and more examples of successful entrepreneurs in your niche, launching new products and services, sharing their wins, and advertising their newest shiny offer. Your brain, doing what it does best, takes this readily available information and uses it to make a quick assessment: "Wow, everyone has this figured out except me. The market is totally saturated. How can I possibly compete?"

This mental shortcut can make it seem like these visible successes are the only stories or the most common outcomes, leading you to naturally conclude that there's no room for your own ideas or contributions. Your brain is trying to help you make efficient decisions, but in doing so, it's actually filtering out a ton of other information that could show you a different picture—a picture where there's plenty of room for your unique voice and vision.

Day-to-day, this lie can be incredibly sneaky. It might stop you from sending that proposal to a potential client because you assume there are better ones out there. It shows up in team meetings when you hold back your ideas, worrying they're not original enough. It creeps into your product development, making you second-guess every choice because something similar already exists. Even in marketing, you might shy away from certain strategies because they've been used by others. Maybe it stops you from starting your dream business to begin with, because you see others thriving in the same niche and assume there's no space for you.

But here's the truth, my friend: while it may be true that there are no new ideas under the sun, the reality is that no one—and I mean no one—can execute an idea quite like *you* can.

Let's break this down because it's essential to recognize why this fear is so limiting and, frankly, why it's not giving you enough credit. Every single person on this planet has a unique blend of experiences, insights, and talents. That means that even if a thousand people started with the same idea, each version would be unique because each person would bring something unique to the table. It's not just about what you do, it's about *how* you do it.

Think about your favorite local cafe or coffee shop. Coffee shops are everywhere, right? But this one, your go-to spot, is special. Maybe it's the ambiance, the way they remember your order, how easy it is to get to, or the super cute server who works on Fridays (hey, no judgment). This coffee shop didn't reinvent the concept of coffee, they just do it in a way that resonates with you personally.

Now, apply that same logic to your business. I'll be the first to tell you that, yes, there are probably at least a dozen other businesses out there doing something similar to what you do. But none of them are going to do it in your voice, with your flair, with your exact blend of magic seasoning. Whether it's your personal story that connects you deeply with your audience, your unique approach to customer service, or your innovative way of problem-solving, what makes your business special is *you*.

Being afraid that "it's been done before" is like saying all the songs have been sung, all the books have been written, all the art has been created. But we know that's not true. Every new song, every book, every piece of art finds its audience and moves people in ways that previous works haven't. Your business, your idea, can do the same.

Wherever you look, on a daily basis there are common, everyday examples of businesses that have rocked the world not because they were the first, but because they brought a unique perspective to a saturated market.

When Apple launched the iPhone, there were already smartphones on the market. However, Apple's unique approach to design, user experience, and ecosystem integration made the iPhone a revolutionary product. Before *Harry Potter* became a global phenomenon, many publishers rejected the manuscript, arguing that the market for children's fantasy books was already saturated. The shapewear industry existed long before Sara Blakely introduced Spanx (we're talking 1300 B.C. here). Despite the *thousands* of years of innovation in the industry, it was her unique approach to product design and relentless belief in her vision that transformed her startup into a billion-dollar business.

To overcome this fear, start by identifying your Unique Selling Proposition (USP). What can you offer that no one else can? This could be your personal service touch, a unique product feature, or an innovative framework.

My mom's container gardens aren't just beautiful, they tell a story of her unique knowledge, care, and creativity. As a mom with a business, we already know a few of your superpowers: multitasking, nurturing, and juggling a million things at once! What else do you bring to the table? Your experiences, challenges, and wins shape your story, and that's something no one else can replicate.

Cross-pollination is one of my favorite business strategies. This concept is all about taking skills and strategies from one area of your life and applying them in a completely different context to create something fresh and innovative. As a mom with a business, you're uniquely equipped to do this because you're already juggling so many different roles and responsibilities every single day.

First things first, recognize that you are a multifaceted individual with a rich history of experiences. You're not just a business owner, you're also a chef, a chauffeur, a problem-solver, a teacher, and so much more. Each of these roles and the other roles you've had in your life have taught you valuable skills that can be applied to your business in unexpected ways.

Let's say you have a passion for photography and you run a home décor business. Why not combine these interests? Use your photography skills to create stunning images of your products for your website and social media. Or, if you're a fitness enthusiast and a life coach, incorporate your love for fitness into your coaching practice by offering wellness tips and exercise routines.

Cross-pollination allows you to bring a unique flair to your business that sets you apart from the competition.

If you're having trouble with this, think first about the skills you've developed as a mom. Are you great at negotiating with a stubborn toddler? Have you mastered the art of delegating chores? Have you developed a skill for simplifying hard-to-understand topics? The patience, resilience, and creativity required in parenting are directly transferable to the business world. You are already a pro at handling complex, dynamic situations.

Beyond your experience as a parent, consider your past job experiences and how they might inform your current business strategies. Maybe you worked in retail and developed a keen sense for customer service, or perhaps you have a background in finance, which can come in super handy when managing your business's budget and financial planning. Every job you've ever had has equipped you with tools and insights that can benefit your business today.

Reflect on challenges you've overcome. Maybe you've dealt with difficult situations that required resilience and determination. These experiences not only shape who you are but demonstrate your ability to persevere and succeed. If you feel comfortable with it, I want to encourage you to share these stories with your audience—they make you relatable and show the human side of your business.

And don't forget about your personal touch. It's the little things that make a big difference. Maybe you include a handwritten thank-you note with every order or remember your customers' preferences and birthdays. These personal touches create a connection and make your customers feel valued.

Cross-pollination is about creative problem-solving. When faced with a business challenge, draw from diverse areas of your life to find a solution. For instance, if you're struggling with marketing, think about how you promote family events or get your kids excited about activities. Those same tactics—enthusiastic storytelling, engaging visuals, and personal connections—will translate to your business audience.

Each skill has the potential to contribute to your business in a distinctive way, even if they are seemingly unrelated. For example, let's say you've always loved baking and have a knack for it. You've spent countless hours perfecting recipes and decorating cakes. This skill can translate directly into a business in a very obvious sense, like a catering service or a bakery. Or, if you want to go for something slightly left of center, it could help you start a blog sharing your baking tips and recipes. But your skills could even serve you in completely unrelated ways, such as using baking metaphors as a business coach or incorporating the practice of baking as a stress-regulating technique as a life coach.

Your passion is another key component of your USP. What gets you out of bed in the morning, even after a sleepless night with a sick kiddo? Your passion is your driving force, and it's infectious. Whatever you're offering, let your passion shine through. When you're passionate about what you do, it's evident in your work and attracts customers who share that enthusiasm. Remember, identifying your USP involves looking at all aspects of your life and experiences. It's about embracing what makes you unique and using that to set your business apart. It's not just about being different for the sake of being different; it's about offering something that only you can provide.

Take Action

1. ***Identify your Unique Selling Proposition (USP).*** What experiences have shaped you? What are your unique skills and talents that may be seemingly unrelated, but could actually come together in a magic mixture that revolutionizes the industry? Write down five experiences that have shaped your perspective and how they influence your work. For example, if you've traveled extensively, how does that cultural knowledge infuse your products or services?
2. ***Connect deeply with your audience.*** The more you understand your audience, the better you can tailor your offerings to meet their specific needs and help them through their pain points. Use your unique perspective to address these needs in ways that others might not think of. Consider creating a survey for your audience to find out their biggest challenges and desires.
3. ***Embrace continuous learning.*** Always be open to adapting, growing, and evolving. Markets change, new trends emerge, and your own needs and desires will shift and clarify over time. Your ability to flex and flow with these changes—not just stick to the old ways—will set you apart. Set aside time each week for learning, even if it's just a few minutes. This could look like reading industry blogs, taking a new course, or listening to a podcast. Keep a journal for quick notes about your new insights and how you might apply them to your work.

4. ***Celebrate your journey.*** Share your story (or as much of it as you want to share) with your audience. People connect with people, not just products. The more of your journey you share, the struggles, the victories, the humanizing moments, the more authentic your brand will feel and the deeper your audience will connect with you. Remember, no one else has lived your life, faced your challenges, or dreamed your dreams.
5. ***Reframe the narrative.*** Reframe how you view the success of others. Instead of seeing other successful businesses as a sign that the market is tapped out, view them as proof that there's a thriving audience for what you want to offer. It's not about the idea being new, it's about the audience needing to hear it from someone like you, in your beautiful unique voice.

So next time that nagging voice whispers, "But that's been done before," shout back, "Not by me!" The world doesn't need another cookie-cutter business, it needs you. With your unique twist on things, who knows how many lives you might touch? You've got something special to offer, so don't let a lie hold you back.

8
I'll Never Get Past This

When I first began writing this book, I discovered I was pregnant with my second child. Let me tell you, to say that it was a complete shock is an understatement, especially since we had thought we wouldn't be able to have kids. In the time it took for that little extra line to show up on the pregnancy test, my entire world got thrown upside down, shaken a bit, spun around faster than my kid spins on the swings, and set back upright again. I hadn't planned on having another child, and this news made me reevaluate every aspect of my life, including my consulting business and my marketing agency, both of which had really started to take off and where I was deeply hands-on with all of my clients. Clearly, things were going to have to change.

Don't get me wrong, I was happy. Being "mom" has always been my favorite title I've ever had and I started to daydream about cute chubby baby thighs and giggles.

I was convinced I was going to have a girl and was envisioning a future where (after some inevitably rocky teen years, of course) we would be best friends. A Rory to my Lorelai.

After a rather rough adjustment period (no doubt made harder by the veritable cocktail of hormones), we started settling into the idea of our expanding family. I adjusted my business plans and started taking the steps to shift my business models to something that would better accommodate the pregnancy, maternity leave, and a new baby. And then the world was turned upside down again. I miscarried as we were entering the second trimester. My identity, already shifting, was thrown into turmoil. I was heartbroken, grappling with immense sadness and an inexplicable and irrational guilt—had I somehow manifested this with my initial fears?

In the wake of the miscarriage, I felt paralyzed. The thought of retracting the business steps I'd started to take during my pregnancy seemed insurmountable. I couldn't bring myself to focus on marketing, emails, or client work. Instead, I found solace lying in the sun. I'd lie down on the front sidewalk, feeling the earth supporting me, the rough texture of the pavement beneath my fingertips, the warmth from the sun on my face, and the sounds of Greyson playing with his trucks next to me. Just letting the simplicity of those moments ground me.

And yet, even as I lay there, the question loomed like a cloud blocking the sun: "How will I ever get past this?"

This lie, the overwhelming feeling of, "I'll never get past this," really digs into the gritty parts of our psyche. It thrives on those moments when you're staring at a mountain of tasks or facing challenges that seem unscalable. This isn't just about having a lot on your plate. Because let's be real, there's always going to be a lot on your plate. It's about feeling as though each item on that plate is a boulder, pushing you down and slowly crushing you beneath its weight as you try to eat it.

Overwhelm is officially defined as a psychological state where the amount, or perceived intensity, of what needs to be managed or resolved feels too great. It's like looking at your daily to-do list and instead of seeing tasks, all you see is a list of fires that you have to put out, each one bigger and more consuming than the last. This feeling usually springs up from a place where your current challenges have piled up to the point that they feel insurmountable, completely overshadowing your ability to envision a solution or even just the next step forward.

Now, let's talk about how recency bias plays into this. Recency bias is a cognitive bias that makes the most recent experiences seem more relevant and significant than they perhaps are. It's like when you have a bad day, it suddenly feels like all you've had is a string of bad days. Have you ever had the thought, "Bad things keep happening to me!" or, "Man, I just can't catch a break!" Chances are, you've had some good things in your life, too. But that recency bias skews your perspective, making it harder to remember when things went smoothly or the many times you've overcome obstacles just like this one.

I'll be the first to admit, that this year started off like a roller coaster—and I'm one of those people who doesn't like roller coasters. Not to throw myself a pity party, but my dog of fourteen years passed away, a water pipe burst in my finished basement causing tens of thousands of dollars worth of damage, my furnace stopped in the dead of winter, my water heater stopped heating water, I got hit with a legal battle, found out I was pregnant, and lost the baby—all within the first four months of the year. *Sheesh*. By the end of April, my emotional reserves were officially depleted and I was left vaguely wondering what progressively horrible thing would happen the next month.

But here's the thing. Amid all those trials, there were also moments of light and positivity. My partner and I grew closer as we navigated the tough times together; the support and love I felt from him were unwavering. Picking out new flooring and paint for the basement (something I'd wanted to do anyway) turned into a fun family project. There were birthdays, anniversaries, celebrations of life, love, and laughter sprinkled throughout.

It can be incredibly hard to see past the valleys when you're in them, and sometimes, you need to sit with your emotions and let them process. But if you only focus on the low points, you'll miss out on the high points that accompany them.

Life's roller coaster can be wild and unpredictable, but it's in those ups and downs that we find our true strength. It's where we learn to appreciate the highs and navigate the lows with courage. So, yes, this year threw me for a loop, but it also showed me just how resilient and resourceful I can be. Remember, it's not about the obstacles we face, but how we choose to see and overcome them.

The truly insidious part of this lie is that believing you'll never get past your current struggles can create a self-fulfilling prophecy of sorts. If you're convinced nothing will change, you'll act in ways that ensure nothing ever does change. If you don't think there's any point in starting to climb that mountain of tasks in front of you, you'll never take the first step, and then you never will climb it. It will just continue to loom over you for the rest of eternity. (Ok, that may be just a *tad* dramatic, but that's the gist of it.)

Maybe you even find yourself hesitating to take on new projects or innovate within your business because part of you fears that these too will become insurmountable challenges. It shows up in how you talk to yourself and others about your business—"I'm just stuck right now" or "I don't see this changing." It can lead to procrastination, a lack of motivation, or even turning down opportunities because they feel like just another chance to fail.

When you don't try out new things because you fear they'll add to your pile of "unmanageables," you're essentially ensuring they *will* by not giving yourself the chance to conquer them. This mindset not only keeps you from progressing but can actually push you backward, as opportunities are missed and potential growth stagnates.

But here's the truth—life is made up of seasons, and just like the most brutal, icy, gray winters give way to spring and sunshine, tough times do change. The key is to hold onto your big, giant, crazy dreams while also acknowledging that every journey is made up of steps—some big, some small, but all important.

If the story isn't good, then it isn't over. Your journey is undoubtedly filled with highs and lows, and every chapter, no matter how tough, is part of a greater story that's still unfolding. Running a business while raising a family is no small feat. There will be days when you feel like you're failing at both. But remember, this is just a chapter, not the whole book. What sets you apart is your perseverance.

And, by the way, while there are some things that are outside of your control, you're not completely powerless. If you're in a chapter that feels like it's going nowhere, take a step back and look at the bigger picture. What's the story you want to tell? How do you want to see yourself in this narrative? You're not stuck in a bad story—you're the author, and you can rewrite the next chapter. Shift your perspective, set new goals, and take actionable steps toward the future you envision.

Amidst the grief after my miscarriage, I began to find clarity. This wasn't just about moving past a personal and professional setback, it was about understanding that life—and business—is cyclical and often unpredictable. We are constantly navigating shifts, and with each turn, we have the opportunity to learn resilience, to find new paths, and to grow. Sometimes the detours lead you to the most unexpected and rewarding of places.

I learned during that time that it's okay to hit pause. It's okay to take time to heal and to be with your family. The business tasks I'd been so worried about falling behind on? They were still there when I was ready to return, and my clients, far from being upset, were supportive and understanding. This period of forced pause helped me to realize that the pressures we place on ourselves to always be moving forward at full speed aren't just unrealistic—they're unsustainable.

In the midst of chaos, it's easy to focus on what's going wrong. Set aside some time daily to intentionally reflect on what's going *right*. It can be as simple as being thankful for a supportive partner, a loyal customer, or even just the ability you have to pursue your passion. Gratitude keeps you grounded and reminds you of the good in your life—and there is so much good.

I know this can be easier said than done, but remember, the journey is preparing you for the destination. Every bump in the road, every setback, every late night and early morning—they're all equipping you with the skills, knowledge, and resilience you need to manage success when it inevitably does come.

Think about it. Have you ever looked back on a tough time in your life and realized it taught you something invaluable? Maybe it was a job you hated that taught you perseverance or a difficult relationship that taught you the importance of boundaries. Each of these experiences added a layer to your strength. A piece to your puzzle, so to speak. Take a moment to reflect on past challenges you've overcome, and look at how far you've come since then! Remember that time when you thought you couldn't handle one more, and then you did? And that moment when you had to seriously think on your feet to come up with a creative solution? Chances are, you've had about a dozen of those moments today alone. You've got this.

Take Action

1. ***Break it down.*** Start by breaking down those big, audacious goals into smaller, achievable milestones. Focus on the next right step, not the entire path. What can you do today, this week, or this month that moves you forward, even if it's just an inch? Even small actions can lead to big changes over time.
2. ***Celebrate wins.*** Make it a habit to celebrate every victory, no matter how small. Completed a task you've been putting off? Celebrate it! Made a decision that's been hanging over you? Give yourself a well-deserved pat on the back. These little celebrations help build momentum and remind you that progress is not only possible, it's inevitable. These celebrations can be as small or lavish as you want; you can take yourself out to dinner, go on a weekend away with your partner, or just gift yourself your favorite snack or dessert (when your kids aren't looking of course, if you don't want to have to share!).
3. ***Embrace the journey.*** I know this can be easier said than done, but remember, the journey is preparing you for the destination. Each challenge equips you with the skills, knowledge, and resilience you need to manage success when it eventually does come. Reflect on past challenges you've overcome and how they've shaped you. Turn the despair into appreciation.
4. ***Live intentionally.*** Focus on how you want to feel, and then work backward to make those feelings a

part of your daily life. Want to feel empowered? Take an action each day that makes you feel in control. Seeking joy? Incorporate moments into your day that bring you pure happiness. This intentional approach to your emotional state can shift your mindset from being stuck to being in motion.

Remember, "I'll never get past this" is just a lie we tell ourselves when we're overwhelmed. With intention, action, and a little bit of grit, there's nothing you can't get past. You can do anything, but you can't do everything all at once. Allow space for a pause if needed, and then focus on just one baby step at a time. It's not about racing to where you need to be or even about feeling that you've lost ground. It's about taking each step as it comes, allowing yourself time to heal and feel what you need to feel, and knowing that sometimes, the most productive thing you can do is to simply allow yourself the space to breathe. From there, you can tackle and build. You'll find that in these moments of pause, you're laying the groundwork for future resilience and success, crafted not despite the setbacks but because of the strength you've forged from them.

By acknowledging this lie for what it is—a distortion of reality—and actively working against it, you can begin to reclaim your power and push forward. Remember, you've gotten past obstacles before, and you will do so again. Have faith in your resilience, embrace your capacity for change, and watch as those walls you thought were impenetrable start to crumble. And on the other side of this challenge is the version of you that's even more fierce and capable than you ever imagined!

9
Wanting Money Makes Me Greedy

When I kicked off my entrepreneurial journey, I set a wild and crazy goal for myself: I wanted to make $50,000 per month. In the circles I grew up in, I may as well have just declared that I wanted to sprout rainbow glitter wings and fly to the moon. The reactions I got from my friends and family ranged from dropped jaws to discouraging advice to lower my sights. Worse, some even whispered that I was greedy—after all, who needs that much money? Isn't that just selfish?

To be honest, those comments shook me. Was I being unreasonable? Should I just aim for something more "modest"? Was I greedy?

Luckily, I didn't pay too much attention to the nay-sayers. Instead, I started stepping out of my usual circles and into new territories. I joined different business memberships, connected online with entrepreneurs from around the world, and started attending networking events that opened my eyes to a whole new world. Suddenly, I was in the company of people who didn't just *dream* of making $50,000 a month, they were *doing* it... and then some! I met a woman who was routinely making $200,000 a month after building a coaching business from the ground up while raising her son alone on welfare, and my perspective shifted entirely. New level unlocked—if she could do it, so could I!

What really blew me away wasn't just the figures they were hitting—it was what they were doing with their wealth. These incredible individuals were using their money as a force for good. They funded scholarships, started charities, built schools in underprivileged areas, supported their partners to quit jobs that didn't fulfill them, and even bought homes for their parents. They were generous, kind, caring, and compassionate.

This experience was a revelation. I learned that making money in itself isn't selfish or greedy. It's a tool—neutral and potent—waiting to be wielded for good or ill. It's about the person holding it. If you're generous, kind, and driven by a desire to make a difference, money amplifies that. It enables you to turn your visions of a better world into tangible actions.

The lie that wanting money makes you greedy is deeply ingrained, but it didn't just pop up out of nowhere. This belief is rooted in what we call money blocks—those sneaky, subconscious beliefs that hold us back and tie our stomachs in knots when we even think about reaching for financial greatness. (And, side note, if you have money blocks, this chapter may already be making you feel a bit squeamish.)

Many of us grew up marinated in sayings like, "Money is the root of all evil," "Money doesn't grow on trees," and, "You have to work hard to earn money." We've seen movies where the wealthy tycoon is almost always the villain, or heard stories painting successful people as greedy or morally bankrupt. These narratives stick, festering in our subconscious, and start coloring how we view money and success and keeping us in a scarcity mindset.

But it's not just old sayings or movies, it's also the cultural scripts we've been handed down. There's this pervasive (and quite damaging, in my opinion) idea circulating in society that being virtuous means *always* putting everyone else's needs before your own, to the point of continual self-sacrifice. This message seems to be particularly aimed at women; we're celebrated for our generosity and willingness to give, yet often judged or side-eyed if we express ambitious desires for wealth.

Mix these elements together—the stereotypes, the sayings, the societal expectations—and you've got yourself one heck of a potent cocktail that can make anyone second-guess their right to want more.

But here's what I want you to know: desiring financial success doesn't just benefit you, it gives you the resources to benefit others. Ask yourself, are these beliefs truly mine, or am I carrying someone else's hand-me-down fears and limitations?

This lie can sneak into your daily decisions and interactions in subtle ways without you even realizing it. Maybe you hesitate to raise your prices to what you truly deserve because you worry it will make you look greedy. Perhaps you feel guilty when negotiating contracts or salaries. Or you might find yourself downplaying your financial goals or successes to avoid seeming “money-focused” in front of friends or colleagues.

Believing that wanting money makes you greedy can lead to a whole host of limiting behaviors. Cognitive dissonance could set in and you might subconsciously sabotage your financial success to align with a more “modest” self-image. Remember when we discussed your blueprint all the way back in Chapter 2? How much money you “should” make is included in this blueprint. If you have a deeply rooted subconscious belief that making more than a certain amount is “greedy,” then guess how much money you’ll end up making?

That’s right—just enough to get by without ruffling any feathers or making anyone think you’re the next Scrooge McDuck.

This mindset can hold you back in so many ways. Not pursuing profitable opportunities, undercharging for your services, or avoiding investments in your business—all because you don’t want to appear greedy. Let me tell you, making money doesn’t make you greedy. It makes you resourceful, smart, and, let’s face it, able to afford that dream vacation you’ve been pinning on your vision board for years.

Imagine you're at a lake, ready to sail out onto the water. If you put your left foot in one boat and your right foot in another, you'll end up going nowhere but down. If your thoughts, actions, and words don't line up, cognitive dissonance will set in and block the flow of abundance.

The truth is, that money is neutral. It's a tool, and like any tool, its impact depends on how it's used. If you use a hammer to smash windows, that's destructive (and usually illegal). But if you use it to build your kids a treehouse, it's constructive. If you are kind-hearted, generous, and caring, more money simply means more resources to amplify those wonderful traits. If you're greedy, well, frankly, that's a character issue, not a money issue.

Think about the positive impacts of wealth. Money can provide security for your family, yes, but it can do so much more. It can create opportunities—scholarships for students who could never afford tuition, seed funding for startups that could one day change the world, support for community services that lift up entire neighborhoods. Whether it's fighting climate change, supporting the arts, or funding medical research, money can help you contribute in meaningful ways to the causes that you care about. When you start to see money as a force for good, as a tool that can help enact change, it shifts your perspective from one of scarcity to one of abundance. From there, you can start to see earning money not as a selfish act, but as a way to further your positive impact on the world. What dreams could you empower? What voices could you amplify?

One practical way to start shifting your money mindset is by practicing gratitude for what you already have. Every day, take some time to jot down three financial things you're grateful for. Maybe it's the payment that just came through, a new client who signed on, or simply the financial know-how you're working on developing. Gratitude turns what we have into enough, and more. It shifts your focus from lack to abundance, which in turn attracts more prosperity.

And then tap into visualization as a tool to help cement your new beliefs about money. Picture yourself using money in positive ways. Imagine funding a community project, taking your kids on a vacation they'll remember forever, or investing in new tools that will help you grow your business. Pair this with affirmations like, "I make good financial decisions," or, "I use money to spread happiness and joy."

Redefining your relationship with money isn't just about personal gain—it's about redefining what wealth means in the context of contribution and community. By changing your own beliefs and actions around money, you not only empower yourself but also set a powerful example for others, especially your kids.

The longest relationship you'll have in your life is with yourself. The second longest? With your money. And your relationship with money can be a mirror of your relationship with yourself. It's like dating, except your bank account is keeping score.

Personally, I never had a problem saving money. As a kid, every single cent of birthday money or hard-earned cash from my lawn-mowing empire went straight into my savings account. But once that money hit the vault, it was on lockdown—and I mean never leaving. I never treated myself to anything, never invested in the things I wanted. As I got older, it became almost a weird hobby to see how far I could stretch a dollar.

Now, don't get me wrong, being frugal isn't necessarily a bad thing. Thanks to my built-up savings and my insanely good dollar-stretching skills, I was able to buy my first house right out of college, even though I was only making nine dollars an hour at the time. But let's be real—frugality can be harmful if it's coming from a place of deprivation... which mine definitely was. By sticking to my basic needs and bare necessities, I was essentially telling myself I didn't deserve anything more.

You know that old saying, "If you want to see someone's priorities, look at where they're spending their money"? Well, the reality for me was that I wasn't spending any money on "extras" that would have made me happy because I hadn't yet prioritized my happiness. I had prioritized surviving, not thriving.

Ultimately, money is only one form of abundance. There's also love, health, happiness, and success, to name a few. By limiting my relationship with money, I was blocking other forms of abundance in my life. At one point, I looked up and found myself with an abundance of money that I had scrupulously scrimped and saved, but I wasn't necessarily *happy*. I was tired, overwhelmed, facing burnout, and thoroughly sick of eating eggs or boxed mac and cheese for every meal. (To this day, eggs still make me a bit sick to my stomach.)

On the business side of things, my refusal to spend more than I "needed" to was forcing me to juggle too many tasks at once and stifling my growth. Instead of investing a few dollars each month into platforms that could help automate my tasks, I insisted on saving the money because I was capable of doing the work myself. This, of course, led to me spending all my time on busy work instead of actually working with clients.

It was an eye-opening conundrum for me. By not spending money, I was blocking my incoming money. Imagine that! I realized I had to shift my focus from a sense of lack—a constant companion my entire life—to a feeling of richness in all areas of my life. No more hoarding pennies and limiting happiness. It was time to invest in myself, my happiness, and my business.

What you have in your life is in direct relation to your thoughts, whether conscious or subconscious. The secret to obtaining whatever you wish is first understanding that you are the master of your life. Your money mindset is no different. Start thinking of money as a tool for creating a richer (and I don't just mean financially), more abundant life. You deserve to invest in yourself and your happiness. True wealth is more than money.

Often, when people think of "wealth," they imagine the material things that represent it. But here's the secret: it's not about the stuff. Instead, shift your focus to the *feelings* those things bring. In Younger Me's visions of wealth, there was always a big, beautiful house. But what was really behind my dream house? A feeling of being centered. The warmth of family, having a place to call "home," and the calm that comes (for me, at least) from having things clean and organized.

But guess what? I didn't need my fantasy five-bedroom lake house with an orchard to start feeling that way. There were other little things I could do to help myself feel centered, warm, and calm right away. Maybe it's a quiet moment to cuddle up on the sofa with my partner, a tidy space (even if it's just *one* toy-free corner of my house), or simply sharing a meal with family.

What can you do right now to feel the emotions of being wealthy and abundant? Take steps to immerse yourself in these feelings, and abundance will flow.

Often, in the quest for abundance, people fall into one of two camps. On one side, you've got the dreamers—those who focus completely on passively manifesting their desires, believing that if they think positive thoughts long enough, wealth will magically appear. On the other side, you've got the hustlers—the "go-go-go!" crowd who endlessly grind and hustle, thinking they can muscle their way to success by sheer force of will.

But here's the truth: true abundance isn't found at either extreme. The magic happens when you find a balance between the feminine and masculine energies inside you—a perfect blend of being and doing.

Feminine energy is all about being. It's about intuitive receiving and allowing, trusting in the process. Think of it as your inner Zen master, the part of you that knows when to pause, reflect, and let things unfold naturally. It's the calm, nurturing side that says, "You are enough just as you are."

On the flip side, masculine energy is about doing. It's molded by action, logic, and reason. This is your inner warrior, the part that sets goals, makes plans, and takes decisive steps forward. It's the driven, strategic side that says, "Let's make things happen!"

When these energies are balanced, you hit the sweet spot of harmony and abundance. Picture this: you're working towards your goals with the strategic, determined energy of your inner boss (that's your masculine side). Meanwhile, you're also allowing yourself to enjoy the journey, trust in the timing, and receive the good things coming your way (that's your feminine side).

When these energies are unbalanced, however, it's like trying to ride a bike with one flat tire. You either feel stuck in inertia, waiting for things to happen, or you're spinning your wheels frantically without getting anywhere meaningful. Neither approach leads to true abundance—instead, they lead to discord and stress.

To find this balance, intentionally merge productivity with self-care. For every task you complete, give yourself a reward. Learn to delegate tasks, and trust others to handle them. Dream big and visualize your goals, but also break them down into actionable steps.

To anyone wrestling with their big, bold financial dreams, remember this: Don't let the world's small thinking tell you what's possible. Don't take on the money blocks of others. Money is not the villain in our stories, it's a vehicle that can drive massive change. Embrace your ambitions, surround yourself with those who uplift your dreams, and use your wealth to leave an imprint of kindness and transformation on the world. You're not just building wealth, you're building possibilities.

Take Action

1. ***Redefine your relationship with money.*** Start by challenging your old beliefs about money. Reflect on the positive impacts of wealth—how it can provide for your family, create opportunities for others, and allow you to contribute to causes you care about. Remember, money is a tool that can be used to do tremendous good in the world.
2. ***Visualize abundance.*** Practice seeing yourself as financially successful. What does that look like? How does it feel? Visualizing success can help you align your subconscious beliefs with your conscious goals.
3. ***Set financial goals.*** Be clear about what you want to achieve financially and why. Connect your financial goals to your values and the positive impact achieving these goals will have on your life and the lives of those around you.
4. ***Talk about money.*** Normalize discussions about money in your circles. Share your goals, challenges, and successes. Talking openly about money can help break down the stigma and allow you to see wealth in a more balanced light.
5. ***Educate yourself.*** The more you understand money—how to make it, manage it, and multiply it—the more empowered you will feel to handle it wisely. Financial literacy is a powerful antidote to money fears and misconceptions.

Remember, wanting financial success isn't greedy, it's a way to ensure security and opportunity for yourself and your loved ones and to make a difference in the world. Embrace your ambitions and let your relationship with money be one of empowerment, not shame. You have the power to create abundance and use it for good, so let's get building wealth without apology!

10
What Will They Think?

Want to hear a secret? There was a time when I was completely paralyzed by the fear of what others thought about me. I was like a chameleon (we just got a book about those at the library), constantly changing my colors to blend in with whoever was around me. Eventually, I even lost track of who I really was.

Every social event felt like I was running a marathon and a half. I spent the entire time holding up a mask, terrified someone would peek behind it and not like what they saw. If there was an empty seat next to me, I'd think it was because nobody wanted to sit by me. If I walked into a room and heard laughter, I was sure it was directed at me.

Flashback to when I was thirteen, on a school camping trip. I trudged up the path to the cabin, focusing on the crunching of the gravel under my hiking boots as I struggled to keep my dad's heavy faux leather bag he took to trade shows on my shoulder. The cabin appeared beyond a bend. I sidestepped a large web with a spider quivering in the middle, gave the bag one last heave, and pushed the door open to reveal my own personal worst nightmare: somehow, I'd gotten assigned to a cabin with the "popular" girls. These said girls were already in the cabin, sitting on the beds, doing each other's hair and giggling, which all stopped abruptly when I walked in. They froze, mid-braid, and looked me up and down, taking in my hiking boots, obvious lack of makeup, and long and very untrendy hair past my waist.

Surprisingly, I managed to make it through most of the week without any major social disasters—until the last day. The final hours at camp found us in the middle of the woods, completing our final group activity: a ropes course. The other students complained nonstop about having to do the course, but not me. I was glad for the escape. Up in the trees, feeling the wind on my face and listening to the birds calling to one another, I felt so much more at peace than I ever did back on solid ground with all the gossip and giggling and stares. And then I heard another call—the call of nature.

Urgently, I climbed down, released my harness, and rushed to the ramshackle bathrooms in the woods near the course. I turned to shut the door but, to my horror, I couldn't get it to close. I leaned against the rough wood and pushed with all my might (and even begged it a bit), but no luck. It remained stuck, leaving a good three-inch gap through which I could see a group of boys glancing toward the bathroom and laughing. Even though I knew they realistically couldn't see much through the gap (and my older and wiser self knows now that they probably hadn't even noticed me), my cheeks burned with embarrassment. All I could think about was their laughter and what they could possibly be saying about me.

I couldn't do it. I left the bathroom, holding it in, wiggling around, trying to focus on anything else, praying for them to hurry up with the buses...but it wasn't enough. With a wave of desperate panic, I felt the warmth spread through my jeans.

There I was, thirteen years old, and I had just peed my pants.

Mortified, I concocted a story about falling in something gross and approached a teacher, hoping to quickly change my clothes. "No. You can't. The luggage has already been loaded on the buses," they told me. I had to endure the entire ride home in my wet, peed-on jeans, trying to ignore the looks and wrinkled noses of the kids sitting closest to me.

And the worst part? (As if it could get worse...) If I hadn't been so caught up in what those few boys might think, I could have just used the restroom and avoided the whole ordeal. I learned a harsh—but valuable—lesson about the cost of letting others' opinions control my actions. It showed me how paralyzing and destructive it can be to care too much about what other people think.

Now, I'm happy to report that I don't really care what others think. Sure, I respect the opinions of my peers and loved ones, but anyone else's opinion of me is, quite frankly, none of my business. I'm unapologetically me, no masks. (If you want proof, I just shared a story about how I peed my pants in Junior High in a very public book.) But let me tell you, it hasn't always been this way. I'm well-acquainted with that particular fear: "What will they think?"

At its very core, this fear tugs at our primitive need for social acceptance and belonging. As humans, we are, and always have been, social creatures. Our ancestors needed their community to survive the wilds of their world, so it's practically baked into our DNA to care deeply about the opinions of those around us.

This need for acceptance and belonging isn't just about feeling popular and liked, it's about feeling safe and secure in our social environments. When we feel accepted, we feel safe. When we feel rejected, it can feel as though our very survival is threatened. This is why criticism or disapproval can sting so painfully, and why we sometimes go to great lengths to avoid it.

In today's world, the stakes have changed a bit. We're no longer battling the elements and fending off wild animals (unless you count dealing with your toddler's tantrum as surviving a wild animal encounter). Instead, we're navigating social dynamics, building careers, and expressing our individuality. Yet our brains still react to social rejection like it's a life-or-death scenario. This can turn the simple fear of "What will they think?" into a significant barrier that prevents you from trying new things, focusing on what is best for yourself, and ultimately growing as an individual.

When you're caught up in worrying about what others will think, you're not living authentically. You may choose business models that look impressive rather than feel fulfilling or speak to your passions. You might stay silent about your brilliant ideas or hide parts of your true self to fit in. It's like wearing an ill-fitting costume every day just to blend in, even though it's uncomfortable and hides who you really are.

This fear often stems from childhood experiences, especially those involving conditional love. If the praise and affection we received as kids were tied to our achievements (like getting good grades, winning at sports, etc.), it could set a foundation for believing that our worth is measured solely by what we do, not who we are. If the message you received was, "You are loved when you achieve," you might have internalized the idea that your value is tied to your success.

This type of conditioning teaches us to perform and conform rather than to connect and express. We learn to wear masks—becoming The Student, The Athlete, The Achiever—not because these roles necessarily reflect our true selves, but because they secure us love and approval. As we navigate through life, the patterns established in childhood don't just magically disappear—they morph and manifest into complex behaviors and fears that can seriously influence our adult lives.

If merely being yourself—quirks and all—wasn't enough to secure love and affection as a kid, you might now find yourself playing a role. You create and wear a mask, showing the world a carefully curated version of yourself that you believe will be more readily accepted and admired. This masquerade can become so second nature that you might even begin to lose sight of where the facade ends and the real you begins.

Imagine waking up every day and putting a paper bag on your head before you leave the house. It's uncomfortable, it's restrictive, it's sweaty, and it probably smells funny. Yet, you wear it because you believe it's the only way to be loved and accepted. But deep down, you know that the real you—the one who snorts when she laughs, or loves horror movies, or has a weird obsession with collecting vintage teacups—is being hidden away, starved of the light she needs to thrive.

But the world doesn't need more masked individuals. It needs you. The real, unfiltered, beautifully flawed you. When you show up as your authentic self, you give others permission to do the same. You create genuine connections and experiences.

Then there's overachieving—the constant pushing of yourself, often in areas of life where you think you'll gain the most approval. This isn't about pursuing your passions or following your joy, it's about proving your worth through your accomplishments. Unfortunately, this often leads to burnout because you're driven by fear rather than genuine interest or happiness.

Overachieving can look like a shiny trophy on the outside—endless accolades, impressive titles, and a packed schedule. But on the inside, it often feels like a hamster wheel, spinning endlessly without any true sense of fulfillment. You keep pushing, striving, and achieving, hoping that one more success will finally make you feel worthy.

But the truth is, worthiness isn't something you earn, it's innate and something you recognize within yourself. It's about understanding that you are enough, just as you are, without needing to prove it through constant achievements.

The fear of what others will think can show up in your day-to-day life in a number of ways. Maybe you find that you hesitate to share your business boldly on social media or in conversations because you're worried about seeming too aggressive or salesy. Maybe instead of celebrating your victories and accomplishments, you find yourself minimizing them to avoid appearing boastful. You could hold back on launching new initiatives or products. There's a chance you're tweaking your personality or your brand to match what you think others want, rather than staying true to your authentic self.

Whenever I work with someone who has anxiety around the thought of what others will think, I say something that may feel a bit harsh at first: Stop being selfish. When you sit and stare at a blank screen, unsure of what to post on social, or hesitate to send an email to your list, or feel uncomfortable sharing what you have to sell, you are focused on your own emotions instead of how you could be *helping* your audience.

Think of it this way: Imagine you're a chiropractor sitting in the park across the street from your office. An older woman joins you on the bench, and after a while, you notice her wincing in pain and grabbing her back. You ask if she's okay, and she turns to you with tears in her eyes, explaining that she has such horrible back pain that she can't even pick up her grandbaby anymore. You can tell instantly what is causing her pain and know how to fix it. Do you just leave her to sit in pain? Or do you tell her that you're a chiropractor and you can help her?

Your hesitation to share your knowledge, your expertise, and your services is the same as leaving that woman in pain. You have the power to make a difference, to alleviate someone's struggle, and to provide solutions that can change lives. No matter what you are selling, what you have to offer is going to have a positive impact on the lives of others. Don't let fear or anxiety hold you back from offering the help that only you can provide. Your audience needs you. They are waiting for your guidance, your insights, and your expertise. Focus on them, not on your fear, and let your passion for helping others drive you forward.

To move beyond this fear, start by recognizing and naming it. Understand that this fear doesn't define you—it's simply a challenge to overcome. Lean into your support network, those who appreciate the real you, and remember why you started your journey. Reconnect with your passion and let it be the force that drives you, not the fear of judgment. And, most importantly, celebrate every step forward, no matter how small, because each step is a declaration that you are more than your fears, and every day presents a new opportunity to be bravely and beautifully you.

Take Action

1. ***Recognize the fear for what it is.*** Start by acknowledging that this fear is a natural human instinct, not a reflection of your worth or capabilities. Knowing why the fear exists makes it less daunting and a bit more manageable.
2. ***Question the "audience."*** Ask yourself, just who are these people that you're really afraid of being judged by? Often, we discover that it's not the whole world, but just a few individuals whose opinions we've drastically inflated in importance. Are these opinions really crucial to your happiness or success? Probably not.
3. ***Focus on your "why."*** Reconnect with why you're doing what you're doing. Whether it's your business, your art, your parenting style, or your lifestyle choices, anchor yourself in your reasons and your values. When you're focused on your personal "why," the fears about others' opinions start to lose their grip.
4. ***Practice vulnerability.*** Vulnerability is courage in disguise. It's showing up and being seen, no matter the risks. The more you practice vulnerability, the more you realize that people's reactions are not in the least bit within your control, and that's okay.
5. ***Surround yourself with support.*** Build a bubble of supporters who lift you up and encourage you. When you have a solid base of people who believe in you, and who love you unconditionally, the negative opinions of others weigh less.

6. ***Show up from a place of love.*** How is what you have to offer going to help others? Write down twenty ways your offer is going to help someone and why they need it and twenty reasons why you are passionate about helping your audience. This will help reframe your thinking away from being focused on your own fears to thinking about the good you're going to do.

So, next time you find yourself paralyzed by "what will they think?" remember, my dear sweet friend, you're here to *live* your life, not to perform it. You are meant to shine in your own unique, quirky way, and the right people will love you for it. Those who mind don't matter, and those who matter don't mind.

11
I Need to Stay Small

When I'm working with a new client, one of the first questions I ask is, "What's your ultimate goal for your business? How big do you want to get? How many people do you want to reach?" And you know what used to surprise me? How many people have the *same exact* answer.

Most of the moms I've worked with who wanted to launch businesses came into it believing they didn't have any choice whatsoever over how big they could get. They thought that they were limited by their schedules with kids, households, and all the mom-life craziness, thinking the best they could do was maybe bring in a couple extra hundred or—if they really hustled—maybe a thousand extra dollars each month.

Here's the reality: if you want to grow an empire that hits six-figure months and reaches thousands of people, you absolutely can. If you want to keep your business small and make extra money to take your family on vacation, that's totally doable too. Whether you're working all day or only during naptime, you have the power to define the scale of your business. You can keep it cozy or stretch it to the skies—there's no invisible script limiting the size of your dreams. The trick is understanding what you want so you can build your business systems accordingly.

Greyson absolutely loves his tumbling classes. Each and every week, we're the first ones at the studio, eagerly waiting for his teachers to arrive. Recently, after finally perfecting his backbend, he officially graduated to the next class level. That meant an upgraded classroom with more advanced equipment, a new curriculum, and more opportunities to showcase his skills. But when I told him he graduated, instead of jumping for joy, he looked up at me with tears welling in his eyes, his little chin quivering, and said he didn't want to graduate. He was scared and wanted to stay right where he was. He was terrified to scale up.

Just like my son, many of us face a very real, very palpable fear of scaling our businesses. It's beyond just scheduling constraints, it's the emotional weight of stepping into a bigger arena.

First up, there's the fear of losing control. As your business grows, there's a very good chance you'll need to delegate more tasks in order to handle your extended to-do list. For perfectionists or for those who have built their business from scratch, this can feel like handing over your baby to a stranger.

Next, there's the underlying fear of exposure. Bigger businesses attract more attention—plain and simple. And with that spotlight comes the fear of public scrutiny and criticism. It's like being the new kid in school again, except this time the whole world is watching. Plus, there are the added fears of legal issues, more complicated tax structures, and the minefield of trademarks and copyright laws. Just thinking about it can make you break out in a sweat. (Still makes me sweat sometimes, if I'm honest.)

And then there's the classic imposter syndrome. As your business expands, you might start to feel like you're not truly qualified to lead a bigger operation. You may doubt your accomplishments and worry about being exposed as a "fraud."

And, if that's not enough, remember, the psychological reasons are only part of the equation. There's also a whole slew of practical reasons that would make it seem impossible to scale a business while also dealing with mom duties. Balancing business growth with family responsibilities can make the idea of expanding seem completely overwhelming. There are resource constraints, whether it's money, time, or emotional and mental bandwidth. And far too often there's a lack of support from others who may not understand your desire to be *more* than just mom.

There's this pervasive idea that moms "should" focus on their families first and foremost, leaving little room for entrepreneurial ambitions. (Society loves to put us in boxes, doesn't it?) But here's the thing: your dreams still matter. You can be an amazing mom and a successful business owner. These roles aren't mutually exclusive. In fact, showing your kids what it looks like to chase your dreams is one of the best lessons you can teach them. Don't let outdated societal norms dictate the scale of your dreams.

Yes, you're balancing playdates, school runs, meal preps, and maybe even the occasional attempt at self-care. It's easy to think, "How on earth could I possibly scale my business with all this going on?" But here's the truth: you're already a master multitasker. If you can wrangle an infant while making dinner and answering homework questions, you can absolutely find creative ways to grow your business. It's not about finding more time, it's about using the time you have more effectively. It's about delegating, automating, eliminating, and prioritizing. Your business *can* grow even if you're only working during naptime.

We all have days when it feels like our emotional and mental bandwidth is maxed out. But remember, you don't have to do it all at once. Small, consistent steps can lead to big growth. Take a deep breath, break down your goals into manageable tasks, and give yourself grace.

If you're caught in the mindset that you have to stay small, it's like placing invisible barriers around your potential. You might find yourself automatically saying no to opportunities that seem too big or too risky. Maybe there's a chance to expand your product line or enter a new market, but you back away, worried it might stretch you too thin. Maybe you hesitate to invest in marketing, new technology, or additional staff that could significantly lighten your daily load and supercharge your efficiency.

Sticking to what you know because it's familiar, even when it's no longer fulfilling or profitable, is a common side effect of this "stay small" mentality. It feels safer to tread water in a pond that's become too small, rather than swim out into a larger lake. But here's the kicker: this "comfort zone" you're clinging to isn't really comfortable at all if it's stifling your growth and zapping your passion. It's just the devil that's known.

When you give in to the idea that you need to stay small, you're not just putting limits on your business, you're limiting your entire life. You create an artificial ceiling that you can't break through, which caps not only your financial growth but your personal development. Over time, this self-imposed limit can lead to a sense of stagnation and leave you more dissatisfied than a toddler wrinkling their nose at a plate of broccoli. You may find yourself haunted by the nagging, painful question of "What if?" What if you had said yes to that partnership? What if you had hired help and pursued that big contract? What if you had expanded when you had the chance?

You risk missing out not only on financial rewards but on the personal fulfillment that comes from pursuing your dreams and realizing your full potential.

To break free from this limiting belief, start by reevaluating your definition of success. Decide what success looks like for *you*, not what Instagram says or what your neighbor is doing, but what genuinely feels right to you. Your vision of success might be a boutique operation that allows you to take afternoons off, or it might be a sprawling enterprise. Right now, I'm in a season where I want to have more time to spend nurturing and pouring into my family and our future, so I've intentionally built businesses that embrace asynchronicity (i.e. I can work on my schedule, not anyone else's) and a one-to-many approach (i.e. capturing my frameworks in group programs or evergreen courses instead of only direct one-to-one work). Whatever *your* vision for your business is, own it unapologetically and ask yourself: what steps can you take to start moving toward your vision?

Begin by setting incremental goals that stretch you beyond your current boundaries... but don't send you into a reeling panic. Think of these as baby steps toward your big dreams. Each small goal you achieve builds confidence and moves you closer to your vision.

Allow yourself to experiment and take (calculated) risks. The path to growth always involves some degree of risk, but these are often the steps that lead to the most rewarding outcomes. Educate yourself. The more you know, the more achievable growth seems. It's like preparing for a marathon—you train, you learn, and then you run. Focus on incremental changes; small, manageable adjustments can lead to big changes over time.

Along those lines, don't be afraid to make (smart) investments in yourself and your business. Whether it's through education, new technologies, or bringing in extra hands to help, these investments can pay off by propelling your growth and reducing your workload. Go ahead and treat yourself to that online course, upgrade your tech, or hire that virtual assistant.

Make sure to recognize and celebrate each step forward in your business growth. We want to build your confidence right along with your business and reinforce that positive growth mindset. Most importantly, surround yourself with a support system that encourages your expansion. Connect with mentors, join business networks, or participate in mastermind groups where you can gain insights and encouragement from others who have navigated similar paths.

Remember, deciding not to stay small doesn't mean you have to become a giant overnight. It means giving yourself permission to grow at a pace that challenges you—without overwhelming you. It's about recognizing that you deserve to dream as big (or as small) as you want and that you have the power to turn those dreams into reality.

Take Action

1. ***Set clear goals.*** Start by defining your vision for your business—with the understanding that this vision is allowed to shift and change as your life shifts and changes. Write down your vision and break your goals down into smaller, actionable tasks.
2. ***Eliminate, Automate, Delegate.*** You can't do everything yourself, and that's okay. Make a list of tasks that drain your time and energy or that don't necessarily need your unique touch. Decide then if those tasks can be eliminated completely or if they can be automated with a tool or software or delegated to a freelancer or new team member.
3. ***Prioritize.*** Along with setting your goals, have an understanding of what your priorities are at this point. What are your non-negotiables day in and day out? Maybe you want to make sure you're always at the bus stop to pick your kiddo up with a snack or you want to take Friday afternoons off for a weekly sister lunch date. Whatever your priorities are, make sure your vision for your business is setting you up for success with them.
4. ***Seek mentorship and education.*** There's always something new to learn! Surround yourself and learn from people who have similar visions for their business so you can mutually inspire and lift each other up! Take it from me, choosing a mentor who has very different business goals from you can lead to a lot of frustration and self-doubt.

5. ***Laugh through the fear.*** Don't forget to laugh. Scaling up is a wild ride, and it's okay to find humor in the chaos. Did your first hire accidentally send an email to the wrong mailing list? Laugh it off and learn from it. Did your new office plant die because you forgot to water it? Consider it a lesson in prioritizing (and maybe get a cactus next time).

Remember, "I need to stay small" is only true if it aligns with your goals and desires. If it doesn't, then it's just another limit you've set for yourself without realizing it. Break those chains, dream big or dream boutique, but always dream in a way that's true to you. You are capable of amazing things, whether on a small scale or a grand one.

12
I Can't Do It on My Own

I used to call my mom for help figuring out which brand of bread to get.

True story.

I'd be standing in the grocery store bread aisle, having a full-on existential crisis over which loaf to buy. Should I get the cheap bread that was kind to my wallet but tasted like cardboard? Or the low-carb bread that was great for my diet but tasted like, well, cardboard? Or the thick, buttery, artisan bread that I loved but was a disaster for both my wallet and my waistline? Eventually, I'd give up and do what every sensible daughter does—I called my mom for her advice.

And—confession time—it wasn't just with bread. (I'm smiling and shaking my head a bit at younger me as I write this.) I'd call her to get advice on whether to buy the cute shoes that I didn't need but were on sale, whether I should make certain investments in my business, whether I should cut my hair... everything.

Eventually, my mama gave it to me straight. "Olivia, you already know what you're going to do. You don't need help. You don't need permission. Just do it."

On the surface, the lie, "I can't do it on my own" might not sound like a lie at all. Help is good, right? Absolutely. But the problem isn't in seeking help (which we'll get into in the next chapter), it's in the belief that you *need* help to achieve success. That somehow on your own, you aren't enough.

The quest for external validation is a road that many of us find ourselves on, often without realizing it. We chase after others' approval, letting their opinions dictate our choices and define our success. But why do we feel the need to look outside ourselves to make decisions or to feel accomplished? It's not just about self-doubt, it's a deeply ingrained habit woven into our psyche through a mixture of early conditioning, relentless societal pressures, and personal fears.

From the moment we're born, we're taught to look to others for approval. Think about it: a child is praised for sharing their toys, for getting good grades, for being polite. These experiences engrain the idea that approval from others equals good behavior and success. This in itself isn't necessarily a bad thing, but if this approval is inconsistent or tied solely to achievements—or if a child is never allowed to make any decisions for themselves—it can lead to those kids becoming adults who don't trust their own judgment. These adults constantly seek validation from others to confirm they're on the right track, doubting their ability to navigate life on their own terms.

And let's face it—nobody likes to fail or face rejection. It stings. It's uncomfortable. For many, the possibility of making a wrong decision and dealing with the consequences is downright terrifying. This fear can be rooted in past experiences where failure led to significant setbacks or harsh judgments. Or it might stem from a general lack of self-esteem, a nagging inner voice that whispers, "You're not good enough." (If that's you, go back and read Chapter 1 again!) Seeking external validation becomes a protective strategy—it's a way to shield ourselves from potential failure and to reassure ourselves that we're making the "right" choice.

But here's the truth, and I need you to lean in and really hear this: You do not need anyone else's approval to validate your worth. Your decisions, your dreams, your passions—they are yours for a reason. The next time you catch yourself looking outside for validation, pause. Take a deep breath. Remind yourself that your value isn't determined by others' opinions. Your worth is inherent. It's time to trust yourself, to believe in your own ability to make choices that are right for *you* and *your* family. Because at the end of the day, the only validation you truly need is your own.

A while ago, I was chatting with another business mom about how she balances her many priorities. She mentioned that it would be absolutely impossible to do without her husband and that you just can't build a successful business without that kind of help. And while

I greatly admired the support and love she felt behind that statement, I'll admit it irked me. Just a bit.

For the majority of my son's life, I've been a solo mom. I didn't have any childcare to speak of and was the sole breadwinner for the family. I was the one changing all the diapers, attending all the business meetings, making all the dinners, fixing all the leaky faucets (seriously, I think every faucet started leaking in my house at the same time one year), and on and on.

Let me be clear—I didn't for one single second resent that she had support from her husband. But her statement that it's *impossible* to build a successful business on your own? That's what didn't sit right with me. I've seen otherwise, both in my own business journey and in the journeys of other single moms running their own businesses.

Don't get me wrong, building a successful business while raising kids and handling the household without support is not easy. It's hard, and exhausting, and trying, and messy, and sometimes a bit lonely—but it's not impossible. And, to be honest, it's an excuse I don't like people to hide behind when it comes to achieving their dreams. It's kind of a pet peeve of mine.

Here's the thing: We often underestimate our own strength and overestimate the necessity of external support. Yes, having help is fantastic and can make the journey smoother, but saying it's impossible without it? That's simply not true. When I started my business, I had no choice but to make it work. I didn't have a partner to rely on, and I certainly didn't have a safety net. What I did have was grit, determination, and a stubborn belief that I could and would succeed despite the odds.

Every diaper you change, every meeting you attend, every meal you cook, and even every leaky faucet you fix can teach you that you are capable of more than you ever imagined. Personally, it taught me that being a solo mom wasn't a barrier to success—it was a powerful motivator. Ultimately, it can push you to find creative solutions, to work smarter and more efficiently, and to keep going even when the going gets tough.

You do not need a partner to validate your dreams or to make them a reality. You do not need anyone else to tell you what you can and cannot achieve. Your success is determined by your drive, your passion, and your willingness to put in the work.

Now I have an amazing partner who is incredibly supportive. At the time of writing this, we're in the somewhat messy and complicated phase of figuring out how/what/when to merge households (which tends to happen when two divorced people with their own kids and houses and pets and far too many extra kitchen appliances meet and fall in love...), but he's there for me for late-night goal-setting sessions, the inevitable moments of self-doubt, and the celebrations of every win along the way. His support means the world to me, and it has added a beautiful dimension to my life. But here's the crucial point: even with his unwavering support, I am still the one responsible for making my dreams a reality. He can cheer me on and lend a helping hand as needed, but the drive and determination to achieve my goals have to come from within me.

The lie of "I can't do it on my own" sneaks into our lives in more ways than we might realize. It shows up in the subtle ways we seek constant approval from others, when we find ourselves waiting for someone else's input or validation before we make decisions or take any action. This can lead to a cycle where you consistently undervalue your own abilities, overlooking opportunities to leverage your strengths because you've become accustomed to relying on others to fill the gaps you believe you have.

When you start to believe you can't achieve success independently, you inadvertently place your dreams and decisions in the hands of others. This dependency can become an unnecessary crutch, hindering your growth and limiting your potential. Every time you hesitate, waiting for someone else to validate your idea, you're not just delaying action—you're reinforcing a belief that your intuition and judgment aren't enough. Over time, this can erode your confidence and obscure your vision of what's possible when you trust yourself.

But the consequences of buying into this lie go even deeper. It can foster a harmful dependency on others, which can be incredibly limiting if that support network is suddenly unavailable or chooses to step back. Imagine you're halfway up a mountain (pretend you're the mountain-climbing type here, if you're not), following a guide through the wild terrain, trusting them and them alone to lead you to the best footholds. Suddenly, the guide disappears and you find yourself all alone. What do you do? If you've never trusted your own climbing skills, the prospect of reaching the summit all on your own can feel impossible. Overly depending on others can erode your belief in your own innate ability to succeed and to solve problems for yourself.

And then there's the potential for resentment—both from you and those you lean on. You might start to feel bitter that you can't move forward without someone else's help, while they might feel overwhelmed by the pressure to always be your support system. Talk about a strain on relationships!

To navigate away from this mindset, you need to start affirming your own capabilities. This doesn't have to be hard or complicated, just start by making small decisions on your own and celebrating those successes, no matter how minor they might seem. Each step you take independently reinforces your ability to stand on your own two feet. Start viewing help as a tool for enhancement rather than a crutch. Think of support as a spotlight that highlights your strengths rather than something that fills in for your weaknesses.

When you embrace opportunities to trust your instincts and take bold steps without waiting for a nod of approval, you can start to dismantle the lie. Celebrate your choices—big or small, right or wrong. Did you make a tough decision without consulting anyone? Fantastic! Did you solve a problem on your own? Incredible! These moments add up, gradually shifting your mindset from one of dependency to one of empowerment.

It's not about shunning support—it's about re-framing it. Support should be like a wind at your back, propelling you forward, not a prop holding you up. Embrace your own power and acknowledge that while guidance, help, and advice from others can be incredibly valuable, your success is ultimately driven by your own actions and decisions. By shifting how you view your need for support, you can start to embrace your own power and truly own your journey to success.

Take Action

1. ***Acknowledge your strengths.*** Regularly take stock of your skills and successes. Remind yourself of what you've accomplished independently and celebrate these victories.
2. ***Seek help as a choice, not a necessity.*** Shift your perspective to view help as a strategic choice for growth and efficiency, not because you lack the ability to succeed on your own. Give yourself permission to make decisions without seeking approval first. Start with small choices (even if it's just picking out a loaf of bread at the grocery) and gradually work up to bigger ones as your confidence grows.
3. ***Develop a support network.*** Build a network not out of necessity but out of the richness it brings to your business and personal growth. This network should empower you, not make you feel powerless without it.
4. ***Set clear boundaries and intentions.*** When you do seek help, be clear about what you need and why. This ensures you're using help effectively and not as a crutch. Change your approach from seeking someone's blessing to seeking feedback. This subtle shift can empower you to trust your own decisions more.
5. ***Invest in personal development.*** The more skilled and knowledgeable you become, the more confident you'll feel in your own abilities. Continuous learning

and development are key to overcoming any potential feelings of inadequacy.

6. ***Tap into your intuition.*** Take intentional breaks to tap into your intuition and get your own guidance on issues you're dealing with. Take a walk, soak in the tub, go for a run—whatever feels best for you to calm your internal monkey chatter and let the truth ring through.

Remember, success isn't about doing it all alone or having help every step of the way. It's about knowing your strengths, recognizing when and where support can amplify your effort, and stepping into your power as a capable, resourceful leader. You are enough, with or without help, and your journey is uniquely yours. Breaking free from the need for external validation isn't about becoming an island unto yourself, but rather developing trust in your own capabilities. Embrace your inner strength, make decisions boldly, and live authentically and confidently, because, at the end of the day, the only approval that truly matters is your own.

13
I Can't Ask for Help

Years ago, I was struck by a wildly ambitious, rather illogical idea. I decided I would run a half marathon. Now, the idea of running 13.1 miles isn't inherently illogical—people do it all the time, right? But here's the catch: I despise running. And not just casually. We're talking a deep, passionate disdain. Plus, I hadn't run a mile since I was forced to in high school gym class. But despite all that, one morning I woke up and decided that I was going to run a half marathon with no training.

(Yes, completely illogical.)

As I've shared throughout this book, it's important to know yourself, flaws and all. One of my little quirks is that I'm headstrong to the core. Once I decide on something, there's no turning back, regardless of the obstacles ahead. This trait has served me well in entrepreneurship and motherhood, driving me to build successful global businesses from scratch. But, as you might guess, it's not always the most *sensible* approach. Case in point: running a half marathon with zero preparation.

It was around mile six of the race when reality hit me hard. I was making my way up one of the many (many, many) hills in the race, my breath coming in ragged bursts and the sound of my shoes slapping against the pavement reverberating in my ears. As I jogged, each step feeling heavier than the last, I wrestled with my decision. Well, that, and the relentless ache in my side that felt like an icepick jabbing into my ribs. I blinked the sweat from my eyes and reached out automatically to grasp hold of a little white paper cup that a kind soul on the sidelines handed me. Inside were Swedish Fish. I hastily bit down on one and instantly wished I hadn't—my already labored breathing now also had to contend with sticky red candy cementing my jaws shut. Yet, with each painful step, a mantra pulsed through my mind: I. Can't. Give. Up. I. Can't. Give. Up.

As I crossed the finish line, tears streamed down my face, in part from sheer exhaustion and pain, but mostly from a profound sense of pride. *I had done it.*

The finish line was a frenzy of costumes, signs, and people cheering at the top of their lungs. I was surrounded by celebration, but none of them were there for me. I had no friends or family waiting for me; I tackled this challenge on my own, and I finished it on my own.

About a month later, I signed up for another half marathon. (See? I told you. Stubborn with a capital S.) This time, though, I approached it with a different mindset.

This time, I met up with my dad every Saturday morning to train. True, our training sessions might have involved more walking than running and typically ended with donuts, but they helped me prepare, both mentally and physically, and—even more valuable— they became our thing. Over the years, those mornings of chatting and walking have morphed into a cherished ritual, with countless miles walked together, and countless memories made. And now, my son gets to join us, too!

I'm not going to lie, the second half-marathon was every bit as physically demanding as the first, but this time *I wasn't alone*. I had support, people cheering for me, and friends waiting at the finish line. The process was still hard, I still got blisters and chafed in awkward places, but the experience in itself was profoundly different. My mantra was the same—*I. Can't. Give. Up.*—but this time, I wasn't the only one chanting it.

I can't ask for help. I can't lean on anyone. I have to do this on my own. I have to prove myself. These lies are far too common, especially for moms with businesses. It's deeply embedded within the fabric of our societal narratives and personal histories. A mindset that's sculpted by cultural idols and childhood lessons, it becomes the heavy as all get-out suit of armor that we wear as adults.

In general, we sure do love a hero's journey—a tale of solitary struggle and triumph that glorifies the "self-made" individual. It's the basic plotline of the vast majority of books and movies out there today: Luke Skywalker's journey from a farm boy to Jedi Knight, Frodo's quest to destroy the ring, Neo's transformation from computer hacker to "The One," Harry Potter's shift from awkward boy to savior of the wizarding world—the examples are endless. (Yes, I know, my geek is showing a bit...)

The hero's journey focuses mainly on, well, the hero. Which, in itself, is an incredibly compelling and inspiring narrative... but it's also profoundly misleading. It suggests that true success is born from isolated effort. But one of the crucial steps in the hero's journey is the "meeting of a mentor," where the hero receives priceless guidance and support from someone else. The heroes may be the main protagonists of their stories, but they by no means are doing everything on their own. Where would Luke be without Obi-Wan Kenobi? Frodo without Gandalf?

For us, this pressure is intensified by the pervasive myth of the "supermom," the elusive creature who does it all, balancing business and family, always drinking the right amount of water and never feeding her kids processed chicken nuggets, all with a smile on her face and nary a drop of sweat on her flawless brow. The message is clear: true strength lies in self-sufficiency, and vulnerability is akin to failure.

Often, we can trace this lie back to our earliest days, to the formative moments of our childhood. If you were lauded for your independence early on, and celebrated for each task you managed on your own, you learned that self-reliance was a prize-worthy endeavor. And if you saw adults in your life consistently eschewing assistance, wearing their independence like a badge of honor, you might have absorbed the message that strong people—successful people—never ask for help. This message, repeated over the years, becomes a cornerstone of your identity, influencing how you navigate both your personal life and your business.

As this belief cements itself in your psyche, it shapes your behavior as a parent and as an entrepreneur. Does this sound familiar at all? You push yourself to the limits, juggling responsibilities with a determined grin, insisting on handling challenges alone. The thought of reaching out for support feels not just uncomfortable but fundamentally wrong, as if it would betray your capability and independence.

I know I've been there! I turned down help walking out of the hardware store, choosing instead to somehow "prove" myself by carrying two gallons of paint in each hand. I changed the battery in a smoke detector on a vaulted ceiling I couldn't reach by stacking three Harry Potter books and a plant encyclopedia on a step ladder. I refused for *years* to hire help in my business, feeling that if I had help, it wouldn't be "my" business anymore and that somehow I would be a fraud. The list goes on and on.

A couple of years ago, I co-founded a new business with a phenomenal woman I met in an online group for female entrepreneurs. Michelle is based in Paris, France (which sounds so much more glamorous than my suburban Ohio locale!) but beyond that, we actually have a lot in common. We are both neurodivergent entrepreneurs, juggling the chaotic yet rewarding task of growing our businesses while raising Littles and living our lives. From the moment we connected, it was like meeting a kindred spirit. We instantly hit it off and embarked on what has become one of the most rewarding experiences of my life.

Working together wasn't just about building a business, it was about building trust and learning to let go of the reins a bit and explore the power of collaboration. Because we each had other business ventures and mom duties, we quickly learned the importance of asking for help when we felt overwhelmed. I cannot begin to tell you how refreshingly liberating it was!

Michelle's partnership allowed me to embrace vulnerability in a way I never had before. It showed me that asking for help is not a sign of weakness but a testament to strength and wisdom. Through this collaboration, I learned that when we open ourselves up to support and trust, we create space for incredible growth and innovation. In fact, sharing the journey with someone just as passionate and driven as I am made the successes even sweeter... and the challenges so much more manageable.

Here's the truth: the relentless pursuit of doing it all on your own is unsustainable and, frankly, unnecessary. It's a breeding ground for burnout, isolation, and inefficiency. It closes doors and stifles the incredible benefits that collaborations and community support can bring to our lives and our businesses.

In the hustle and bustle of everyday life, the lie of "I can't ask for help" often leads us down a challenging and exhausting path. Many of us find ourselves trying to juggle it all—balancing the intense demands of running a business with the equally consuming tasks of family life. This drive to manage everything solo can make us hesitant to delegate, even when it's clear we can't do it all by ourselves. It's not just about being busy, it's about proving—to ourselves and others—that we can handle it all. This mentality often leaves us feeling isolated, as if we've marooned ourselves on an island and refuse to signal to any of the passing ships that could save us.

But let's talk about the real consequences of buying into this lie. First, there's burnout—the complete exhaustion that comes from trying to carry too much on our shoulders. It's the physical and emotional fatigue that sinks in when we refuse to acknowledge that we need support. Burnout isn't just a fleeting moment of tiredness, it's a debilitating state that can rob us of our passion, creativity, and joy.

Then, there's the impact on our businesses. By not leveraging the strengths and skills of others, we limit our companies' abilities to grow and thrive. We miss out on opportunities for innovation and expansion because we're too caught up in the minutiae of daily operations. Our businesses become stagnant because we're trying to be the superhero who does it all, instead of the visionary leader who empowers others to shine.

Our relationships also suffer under the weight of this lie. When we insist on handling everything ourselves, our partners, family members, and colleagues can feel pushed away and undervalued. They might want to help, to share the load, but our insistence on independence can create a barrier that leaves everyone feeling disconnected. The people who love us want to support us, and by not letting them in, we deny them the opportunity to be part of our journey.

And let's not overlook the decrease in effectiveness that comes with trying to multitask without support. The truth is, that multitasking often leads to more mistakes, less creativity, and slower progress. Each task gets only a fraction of our attention, and the quality of our work suffers as a result. We spread ourselves too thin, and instead of excelling in one area, we end up mediocre (at best) in many.

Here's the reality check: Asking for help isn't a sign of weakness, it's a mark of wisdom. It doesn't mean you're incapable, it means you're smart enough to recognize that your time and energy are finite resources that should be invested wisely. It shows that you understand the value of collaboration and the strength that comes from community, and are ready to elevate your business and personal life by building a network of support. By reaching out for support, you're not only lightening your load but also creating opportunities for others to contribute their unique talents and perspectives.

I also understand that the fear of asking others for help could stem from a time when you did actually muster the courage to ask for help, only to be let down, betrayed, or hurt. It's a gut punch, for sure. A pain that lingers far longer than we'd like to admit. And from that moment on, the fear sets in—a fear that asking for help will always lead to disappointment and that it's safer to go it alone than to risk being let down again.

But this is just a story we tell ourselves to protect our hearts from the pain of past wounds. It's well-intentioned, but just a story nonetheless. Yes, someone might have wronged you before. Maybe you trusted someone, and they didn't come through for you. Maybe you leaned on someone, and they let you fall. But not everyone is that person, and your past does not dictate your future.

Holding on to this fear is like walking through life with a shield up, blocking not only the potential hurt but also the incredible opportunities for support and connection. It's a defense mechanism that keeps us isolated, burdened by the weight of trying to do everything ourselves. We think we're protecting ourselves, but in reality, we're just limiting our growth and potential.

The key is to ask for help with discernment. Learn from the past, but don't be imprisoned by it. Look for people who have proven themselves trustworthy, who align with your values, and who show up consistently. It's about building a network of support that is based on mutual respect and reliability.

So, how do we move past this lie? It starts by recognizing that asking for help is a strength, not a weakness. It involves redefining what it means to be competent and successful. It's not about doing it alone, it's about building a network of support that allows you to bring your best self to every aspect of your life. You can begin by asking for help with small tasks, gradually increasing your comfort level with sharing responsibilities. You can communicate openly with loved ones and colleagues about your needs and challenges, and you can seek out communities of like-minded individuals who understand the pressures and rewards of balancing work and family life.

Take Action

1. ***Acknowledge your needs.*** Start by acknowledging that it's human to need help. Just recognizing this in itself can be liberating and is the first step toward change.
2. ***Reframe asking for help.*** Shift your perspective to view asking for help as a strength. It shows foresight, planning, and the ability to collaborate—key skills for any successful entrepreneur.
3. ***Start small.*** Begin by asking for small favors or delegating minor tasks. This helps build your comfort level and trust in others' abilities.
4. ***Build a support network.*** Cultivate a network of peers, mentors, and friends who understand the entrepreneurial journey, and the journey of running a business while raising kids. Regular interaction with this community can normalize the practice of seeking and offering help.
5. ***Celebrate team achievements.*** When you do ask for help, celebrate the successes that come from collaboration. This not only reinforces the value of teamwork but also shows gratitude to those who assist you.

Remember, asking for help is not a betrayal of your capabilities. Rather, it's an affirmation of your determination to succeed. No one truly does it alone, nor should they have to. The most impactful stories of success are those that include chapters of collaboration, support, and mutual growth. Lean into these truths and allow yourself the grace and strength to ask for help when you need it. Being headstrong and independent are qualities of mine that I like, but learning to embrace help doesn’t diminish our strengths—it amplifies them. We are stronger together. Whether you’re running your business or a half marathon, remember that it’s okay to lean on others.

14
I Can't Say No

When I was fresh out of college, I worked at a local plant nursery (just like my mom!). Horticulture is very much in my blood. Though the work was incredibly physically demanding and I could have *very* happily done without the long hours spent in the snow taking cuttings every winter, I loved it. I loved the plants, nurturing and helping them grow, the peace and quiet, not to mention how blonde and tan I got working out in the sun every day! What I didn't love so much was the people aspect.

There was a group of women there who were continuously grumpy, cantankerous, and downright mean. When I first started, I was shocked to be met with a slew of gossip about me. As I worked my way into leadership roles, the gossip and rumors became even more vicious. Eventually, what had once been excitement and passion for my work turned into a ball of dread in the pit of my stomach. I cried at work almost daily; I couldn't for the life of me understand why they were so darn *mean* to me. I tried to be friendly and kind to everyone: what had I ever done to them?

Years later, I can look back and understand that it had very little to do with who I was and everything to do with their own perspectives. The work at the nursery was hard, the elements unforgiving, and the pay was paltry, at best. Most of those women had worked at the nursery for years. When this fresh-faced, ambitious young whippersnapper came in and quickly moved up the ladder, it ruffled a few feathers.

For years, I worked at the nursery, waking up each morning dreading what was to come. We were in the middle of the Great Recession, and I had been told I should just be happy to have a job, even one in a toxic environment that I had grown to hate. And then one day, I had an epiphany.

One spring morning, I walked into the office to grab a new pair of pruners, and it hit me. On the rough wooden wall, there was a sign, covered in years' worth of dust and grime, that read, "What you tolerate, you teach." I'd seen the sign a million times, but for some reason, that morning, it struck a chord. I didn't want my life to look like this. I didn't want to be treated this way. And yet, I had done nothing to change it.

Whether it's within our homes, our businesses, or our communities, our actions—and sometimes our inactions—establish standards. They teach those around us what is acceptable and what isn't. We teach through every choice we make and every behavior we accept from others and from ourselves. We're constantly setting expectations, often without even realizing it. If you consistently accept less than you deserve, you're teaching everyone around you—including your children, colleagues, friends, and most importantly, yourself—that these compromises are okay. This might manifest as tolerating disrespect, accepting subpar performance, or repeatedly letting your boundaries be crossed.

I had stuck around at a job that drained me of every last bit of hope and positivity faster than my kid sucks down juice boxes at Papa's house, all because I had been scared to say no to the "opportunity." But that morning, I decided to put my foot down, establish my boundaries, and start looking for another job.

Within a week, I found one that paid double what I was making at the nursery, had benefits, and didn't require me to spend any time in the snow whatsoever. That job turned into a stepping stone on the path to launching my own businesses and finding this feeling I have right now—that I am truly living my purpose.

Every now and then, I wonder if I ever would have found this feeling if I hadn't made the decision to say no and establish my boundaries all those years ago. That moment was a pivotal point in my journey. It taught me that we have the power to change our circumstances, to refuse to tolerate what doesn't serve us, and to set the standards for how we want to be treated.

It can be incredibly challenging (to say the least) to say no to things. Whether it's turning down a new project because your plate is already overflowing or denying your puppy-eyed toddler that pre-dinner cookie, the struggle is real. Many of us grew up in environments where we were subtly (or not so subtly) taught to prioritize pleasing others. We were led to believe that saying yes was synonymous with being accommodating, likable, and capable.

These deeply ingrained habits can make you feel like you have to always be agreeable, regardless of the personal or professional cost. And let me tell you, when it comes to running a business, this mindset can really throw a wrench in your growth. It's tempting to think that you need to seize every single opportunity that comes a-knocking—every collaboration, every speaking engagement, every new client proposal. It feels like saying no might shut a door forever, or make you appear ungrateful or unambitious. But here's the truth: *not every opportunity is the right opportunity.*

When you're building something important—be it a business, a family, or a balanced life—you have to be strategic about where you invest your energy. Saying yes to everything isn't just unrealistic, it's unsustainable. It dilutes your efforts and distracts you from your goals. You end up stretched too thin, and what was meant to be a path to success becomes a fast track to burnout.

Let's talk about boundaries. Boundaries are the invisible lines we draw around ourselves to protect our time, energy, and well-being. They're the rules we set for how we want to be treated by others and how we choose to engage with the world, and are essential for maintaining balance and avoiding burnout. And yet, so many of us struggle to set them, let alone enforce them.

Imagine trying to drive a car without brakes. You'd be careening down the highway, unable to stop or slow down, constantly at risk of crashing. That's what life without boundaries feels like. You're saying yes to everything, trying to do it all, and eventually, you're going to hit a wall—hard. Boundaries are your brakes. They give you the power to slow down, to stop when you need to, and to navigate all of life's little twists and turns with confidence and as much control as possible.

Setting boundaries starts with understanding your own needs and values. What's important to you? What are your non-negotiables? For some, it might be time with family. For others, it could be personal time for self-care, or the ability to work without constant interruptions. Whatever your priorities, boundaries help ensure that those needs are met.

But let's get real for a moment. One of the biggest reasons we avoid setting boundaries is fear. Fear of disappointing others, fear of conflict, fear of being seen as selfish. But boundaries aren't just about saying no to others—they're about saying yes to yourself. When you set a boundary, you're making a commitment to honor your own needs and values. You're saying, "Hey, I matter. My time and energy are valuable, and I am choosing to protect them."

Actually, I think *not* setting boundaries is what truly leads to disappointment—disappointment in ourselves for not standing up for what we need. Think about it. How many times have you said yes to something you didn't want to do, only to feel resentful and drained afterward? How often have you sacrificed your own well-being to keep the peace, only to find yourself overwhelmed and burned out? Boundaries are the antidote to this cycle of self-sacrifice. They empower you to take control of your life, to make choices that align with your values, and to create a sense of balance and fulfillment.

But I also know that you're a mom, and as such you're probably the go-to person for everyone else's needs, which can make enforcing boundaries challenging. But it's essential to remember that setting boundaries isn't about shutting people out—it's about letting the right people in, on your terms. It's about creating healthy, respectful relationships where your needs are just as important as everyone else's. And in doing so, you'll teach those around you, including your kids, how to set healthy boundaries for themselves.

Here's a tip: Start small. You don't have to overhaul your entire life overnight. Begin with one area where you feel overwhelmed or undervalued. Maybe it's with your business, where you're constantly working late to finish projects. Or your home life, where you never have a moment to yourself. Identify one small boundary you can set, and practice enforcing it. Maybe it's setting an "end time" to your day, or taking fifteen minutes for yourself every afternoon. Gradually, as you become more comfortable with setting boundaries, you can expand them to other areas of your life.

Every single day, we're faced with countless choices. Do I say yes to this new business collaboration? Do I commit to that friend's party this weekend? Do I invest my time in learning a new skill or do I give my mind a rest and binge-watch something instead? These decisions might seem small in the moment, but each one is a little fork in the road that can either lead you closer to your goals or divert you away from them.

Being mindful of your long-term goals means you need to get real about what truly matters to you. When you're clear on your goals, deciding whether to say yes or no to things becomes a whole heck of a lot easier.

Think about it like this: Your time and energy are your most precious resources. (Maybe even more precious than your favorite concealer and morning coffee...) Every time you say yes to something, you're saying no to something else. If you're constantly saying yes to things that *don't* align with your goals, you're spending your resources on distractions rather than your dreams.

Imagine your goal is to write a book. You've dreamed about it for years, and you know it's something that will bring you immense fulfillment. But every time you have a free moment, you're saying yes to activities that have nothing to do with writing. Lunch dates, scrolling through social media, binge-watching TV shows. None of these things are bad on their own, but if they're *consistently* pulling you away from your writing time, you're not aligning your decisions with your goals.

Being mindful of your long-term goals means you need to become the gatekeeper of your time. It's about evaluating every opportunity that comes your way and asking yourself, "Does this bring me closer to my goal, or does it pull me further away?" It's about learning to say no without guilt because you understand that every no is actually a yes to something that truly matters. Every successful person you admire has mastered the art of saying no to good things so they can say yes to great things. It's about prioritizing your dreams over immediate gratification. It's about playing the long game.

Now, I get it. Saying no can be hard. We don't want to disappoint people or miss out on fun opportunities. At its core, people-pleasing is all about seeking approval and avoiding conflict. We want to be liked, to fit in, and to be seen as kind and helpful. I'm not saying these desires are bad at all, but when they take over, we start to prioritize others' needs above our own.

A lot of people-pleasing stems from our upbringing and societal conditioning. From a young age, we're taught to be polite, to share, and to put others first. While these are valuable lessons, they can also morph into an unhealthy pattern of constantly seeking validation from others (flashback to Chapter 12). Add to that a dash of fear of rejection or conflict, and there you have it, folks—the perfect recipe for people-pleasing.

The first step to overcoming a people-pleasing tendency is awareness. Start by recognizing when you're people-pleasing, and then dig into why. Are you afraid of disappointing someone? Do you feel guilty saying no? People-pleasing often comes from negative beliefs about ourselves—like thinking we're not good enough unless we're making others happy. Challenge these thoughts. Remind yourself that your worth isn't tied to how much you do for others.

From there, work to set up those healthy boundaries! Be honest with yourself about your capacity, needs, and priorities. Surround yourself with people who respect your boundaries and support your growth and your dreams of creating a life that feels fulfilling.

Let's talk about that a bit. What would it be like to have a life that feels fulfilling and in flow? When you wake up excited for the day, your actions align with your values, and you feel a sense of ease and joy more often than not? This isn't just a dream—it's a reality that you can and *are* creating by making intentional choices and setting clear boundaries.

We see a lot of successful and productive women. We also see a lot of anxious, afraid, and apologetic women. But how often do we see relaxed women who are at ease, who aren't afraid to prioritize their needs, whether it's rest, play, pleasure or progress? Who give themselves unconditional permission to let down their hair and do what they choose to do without a feeling of guilt or like they need to earn it? That's the kind of woman I aspire to be, and I hope you know that it is possible for you, too.

Take Action

1. ***Recognize your worth.*** Understand that your value does not decrease because you set boundaries. Saying no does not make you a bad mom or a poor business owner, it makes you a wise one.
2. ***Practice different ways to say no.*** Saying no doesn't have to make you a meanie pants. You can say no directly or gently, but it's always clear. To others: "I appreciate you thinking of me, but I can't commit to this right now." To overcommitting: "My schedule is full, but let's touch base next month." To yourself: When tempted to break your own rules (like working late nights), remind yourself, "No, I cannot chase that distraction right now. I need to focus on this because..."
3. ***Understand that no is a complete sentence.*** You are not required to justify, argue, defend, or explain your decisions.
4. ***Build a support network.*** Surround yourself with other entrepreneurs who understand the importance of boundaries. Their support can reinforce your resolve and provide practical advice on how to maintain boundaries when you're tempted to break them... or even just bend them a teensy bit...
5. ***Reflect on your yeses.*** Regularly evaluate the things you've agreed to. Are they serving your goals, or are they distractions? This reflection time can help you make more aligned decisions moving forward.

Living in flow means aligning your actions with your true self. It's about finding that sweet spot where your work, your passions, and your personal life harmonize. It's not about being busy, it's about being intentional. When you're in flow, you're not just treading water, trying to stay afloat. You're *thriving*. You're doing the work that lights you up, spending time with the people who uplift you, and making space for rest and joy.

One of the most powerful tools for creating a fulfilling life is the ability to say no. No to the obligations that drain you, no to the commitments that don't align with your goals, no to the endless to-do list of busy work that leaves you feeling exhausted and unfulfilled.

Say no so you can say yes—yes to yourself, yes to your dreams, yes to your well-being and the well-being of your family, yes to a life that feels rich and meaningful and deep.

You have the power to rewrite your story. You are not defined by or beholden to the lies that you've been told or even the limitations you may have imposed on yourself in the past. You are a fierce, capable, extraordinary woman, capable of achieving anything you set your mind to.

Remember, you're not alone on this journey. I'm here for you, and there is a community of women just like you—moms who are juggling businesses, families, and personal growth—who are cheering you on.

And as you move forward, hold on to the truths you've discovered. You are worthy of success. You can have it all—whatever all means to you. You can be an amazing mom and a thriving entrepreneur. Your dreams are valid, and your path is yours to create. Don't let anyone tell you otherwise.

So, the next time you find yourself doubting your abilities or feeling overwhelmed by the demands of life, take a deep breath. Stand tall, pop that baby on your hip, and step confidently into the life you deserve.

You are unstoppable. You are extraordinary. And your journey has only just begun.

So go get it, mama!

Conclusion and Resources

Though each of these lies can show up differently at different times in your life, there is one common thread that weaves throughout each: fear.

Fear is a powerful force, to be sure. (Not *quite* as powerful as a stampeding three-year-old, but pretty darn close...) Fear can hold you back, whisper lies that keep you small, and create invisible barriers to your vision of success and happiness. But here's the thing: fear doesn't have to be the enemy. As we've discussed, fear can be more of a guide, a teacher, and even a friend if you learn how to understand it and harness its energy.

Let's start with a fundamental truth: fear is natural. It's a biological response designed to keep us safe. Anxiety and fear are woven into the fabric of our beings, and it's not just something you can tell yourself to "get over." Most of our fears won't just disappear overnight—and that's okay. And some of us (like me!) are wired to feel fear and anxiety at higher levels than others—that's also okay. There is no more shame in feeling fear than there is in feeling love, happiness, sadness, guilt, or any other natural human emotion.

The other day in church, the pastor was discussing the phrase "do not fear," which apparently appears a whole lot in the Bible. But the phrase doesn't mean that you shouldn't ever experience fear—it means don't let fear control your life. The goal isn't to eliminate fear but to coexist with it in a healthy way.

To me, that means trying to understand what is behind your fear. Which of the lies we talked about resonate most with you—where are your deepest fears? You have to name it to tame it. Vague fears are much scarier than specific ones, and almost impossible to dismantle.

So, how is your fear trying to help you? Often, fear is trying to protect you from perceived harm. It's your brain's way of saying, "Hey, be careful!" But we need to differentiate between actual real danger and perceived threats to our ego or comfort zone. Fear isn't inherently bad—it's a signal. It's telling us that something matters, that we're stepping into territory where we have the chance to grow.

So grow! Ask yourself: What is the worst that could happen? Plan for it. When you confront your worst-case scenario, you often realize it's not as catastrophic as your mind made it out to be. Now, flip the script: *What is the best thing that could happen?* Often, our brains are so caught up in their own little doomsday scenarios that we forget that there are amazing rewards to be had for facing our fears.

Have the courage to lean into fear. Acknowledge it. Say to yourself, "Yes, I'm scared, but I'm going to do this anyway." Remember, you are not a fearful person—you are a really freaking strong person who sometimes feels fear. Be careful how you label yourself. We all fear something different, but we're not alone in our fear. We all experience it.

Whether you're scared you're not enough, that you're a bad mom, that you're going to fail, that you can't do this on your own, or any other combination of any of the lies in this book, you can and you *are* in the process of understanding and overcoming those fears. The fact that you picked up this book in the first place is testament to that.

For additional free resources to help you on your journey (including an audio imprint to help you break through any subconscious barriers you may have, a checklist of all the action items from the book, and a super handy guide for those who are trying to support you on your journey, and more!), visit www.holdmyjuiceboxbook.com.

I want to thank you from the absolute bottom of my heart for allowing me to be part of your journey. Now I want to hear from you! If you have any takeaways, stories, or just want someone to chat with about your journey as a mom with a business, send me a note at: olivia@thebluebellgroup.com.

Remember, the only limits are the ones you set for yourself. Keep dreaming big, keep pushing forward, and keep on being *you*!

Acknowledgments

"Be strong, be fearless, be beautiful. And believe that anything is possible when you have the right people there to support you."

— Misty Copeland

This book, along with so many other things in my life, would not have been possible without the brilliant support, contribution, collaboration, encouragement, and sometimes tough love of some amazing humans that I have been blessed to have crossed paths with.

To Greyson, first and foremost, thank you for being the best son a mom could ask for. Day in and day out, you inspire me to be a better person. Thank you for helping me find my purpose in life.

To Mike, thank you for believing in me, loving me, pushing me, sitting for hours listening to me read chapters until I was hoarse (and then making me tea to help...), for giving it to me straight and never sugar-coating feedback, and for distracting me and making me smile whenever I get a little too lost in my head.

To Mom, Dad, Erica, and Paul, I could not have asked for a more supportive family. No matter what, through every part of my journey (and let's be real, there have been some pretty rough parts...), you have always had my back.

To Willie, I don't know if I can ever tell you how much your unconditional friendship and support have meant to me over the years. Thank you for reminding me to sometimes let Olive out.

To Michelle, thank you for showing me that it's okay to embrace the neuro-spicy, to lean on others for support, and to actually hold boundaries for myself. (And thanks for holding them for me when I forgot!)

Thank you to the amazing group of friends and colleagues who agreed to act as guinea pigs and read the (very) rough first drafts of this book: Cheryl, Fonda, Alankrita, Smita, Jenna, Rayna, Caren, Moneke, and Jess, and to all my biz besties who were vulnerable and helped share your stories and experiences as fellow moms with businesses so that I could speak directly to the lies that plague us the most.

And to you, dear reader, I am so grateful for the generosity of your time, attention, and heart. May your business and personal growth be exponential, your dreams endless, and your nap times peaceful.

About the Author

Olivia Radcliffe is an award-winning business and marketing strategist and founder of The Bluebell Group. She helps moms grow their businesses (even if they only have naptime to work in!) and is passionate about helping people find their authentic selves and live purpose-driven lives. Olivia is a bestselling author and co-host of the *Marketing Like a Mother* podcast. She lives in Ohio with her son, Greyson, partner, Mike, and bonus kiddo, Jayden.

Get Connected: thebluebellgroup.com

Olivia is available for select readings and speaking engagements. To inquire about a possible appearance, please email hello@thebluebellgroup.com with details.

www.ingramcontent.com/pod-product-compliance
Lightning Source LLC
LaVergne TN
LVHW010741170826
845671LV00053B/402/J

* 9 7 8 1 9 1 5 7 7 1 9 8 8 *